Life & Loss

Second Edition

LIFE & LOSS

Second Edition

A Guide To Help Grieving Children

Linda Goldman

Accelerated Development Inc.

Publishers

Philadelphia • Pennsylvania

USA	Publishing Office:	ACCELERATED DEVELOPMENT *A member of the Taylor & Francis Group* 325 Chestnut Street Philadelphia, PA 19106 Tel: (215) 625-8900 Fax: (215) 625-2940
	Distribution Center:	ACCELERATED DEVELOPMENT *A member of the Taylor & Francis Group* 47 Runway Road, Suite G Levittown, PA 19057 Tel: (215) 269-0400 Fax: (215) 269-0363
UK		ACCELERATED DEVELOPMENT *A member of the Taylor & Francis Group* 11 New Fetter Lane London EC4P 4EE, UK Tel: +44 171 583 9855 Fax: +44 171 842 2298

Life and Loss: A Guide to Help Grieving Children 2nd Edition

3 4 5 6 7 8 9 0

Printed by Sheridan Books—Braun-Brumfield, Ann Arbor, MI, 1999.
Cover design by Judith Kahn and Joan Wendt
Edited by Hilary Ward and Dina Direnzo

A CIP catalog record for this book is available from the British Library.
∞ The paper in this publication meets the requirements of the ANSI Standard Z39.48-1984 (Permanence of Paper).

Library of Congress Cataloging-in-Publication Data

Goldman, Linda, 1946–
    Life & loss : a guide to help grieving children / Linda Goldman. —
2nd ed.
      p.   cm.
    Includes bibliographical references and index.
    ISBN 1-56032-861-4 (pbk. : alk. paper)
      1. Grief in children.   2. Loss (Psychology) in children.
3. Children—Counseling of.   I. Title.   II. Title: Life and loss.
BF723.G75G65   1999
155.9'37'083—dc21   99-36242
                                                              CIP

ISBN 1-56032-861-4 (paper)

This book is dedicated to the children of the world

and to the child within each of us.

Table of Contents

Preface: A Global View of the Grieving Child

The New Millenium is upon us, and its arrival brings us a responsibility to meet the ever changing needs of future generations of our children. Today's children, and those of tomorrow, are grieving children. These children are not only those who have had lost a toy, a pet, or a parent, but are also the majority of our existing young people.

The world and our daily lives are changing rapidly. Children have become fearful of life circumstances that most of us as children never dreamt of. Guns, AIDS, terrorism, murder, suicide, and abuse are all too present in their awareness. TV brings distant terror into our home and graphically imprints it onto our children's vulnerable, innocent minds. The prevalence of violent entertainment and news coverage creates a sense of normalcy and realism that is all-invasive. Thus children feel unprotected by the adult world, and their safety in school, outside the home, and even inside their home feels threatened. Their ability to visualize a future is becoming more limited. Our concern for our children's school performance and social and emotional well being needs to address the huge, hidden realm of life issues that distract and preoccupy their thoughts and feelings.

Children's grief is not the isolated problem of loss-identified children. Children's grief is endemic—it is global. Our goal is to learn to identify this grief and work with it constructively. We need to protect and prepare our youth to live in their world, and make it our world too. As long as we deny their grief issues, our kids will feel alone and at risk. By our acknowledgment of their losses, children will feel we are affirming their reality. One of our primary challenges is to recognize the breadth and scope of the issues revolving around our grieving children and the interrelationship between unresolved grief, educational success, and responsible citizentry.

In beginning to lay the groundwork, parents, educators, therapists, clergy, physicians, and all caring professionals need to take a fresh look at the present model used for mental health and learning. Acknowledgment of the relationship between repressed grief, ability to learn, and self-growth is essential. The emergence of a therapeutic educational paradigm for the grieving child based on this obvious connection has been slow in coming.

This new paradigm that relates quality of learning to the shutdown of traumized children needs to be brought out into the light of day. Let's look at today's world—today's needs, today's children—with a new way of seeing.

Children, parents, and professionals need to receive comprehensive trainings, resources, and supports to work with the groundswell of today's grief and loss issues. Only then can we create a global grief community capable of safeguarding our youth in the twenty-first century.

Too often, unresolved grief in children not only leads to an inability to learn, but also results in overwhelming and powerful emotions that get trapped. All too frequently, in destructive ways. Young people project on the world their unrecognized grief feelings in the form of homicide, violence, and abuse, or they project on themselves these blocked emotions, culminating in self-hatred and possible suicide ideation and completion.

The future of America and the world rests on creating tomorrow's citizens that do not become the criminals, the homeless, or the drug addicted. If young people carry unacknowledged grief issues to such an extreme, they can become a detriment to themselves as well as society. Unfortunately, this is the path of all too many of today's youth. As we enter the millenium we need to produce a citizenship capable of carrying mankind safely through the next thousand years.

Creating a society of productive human beings demands work. This work includes using evolving systems that allow a child's grief to be expressed itself rather than to be repressed. Only then can the inner growth of the child light the way to his emotional maturity, inner wisdom, and responsible place as a citizen of the world.

Introduction

This book is written for and about children. It is also written for and about adults who want to help kids work through their issues of loss and grief. As a mom, stepmother, teacher, therapist, and educator, I am very aware of the importance of open communication, expressing feelings, and access to helpful resources during sensitive times in a child's life. My goal is to create a guide that empowers parents, educators, clergy, and health care professionals to handle children's loss and grief issues in an informed, open, and loving way, reducing the fear and denial often associated with these topics.

 Each chapter of this guide includes suggestions that allow the mind, heart, and common sense to work together to create a caring environment for kids.

This guide is user friendly. One can open to any page and find useful information. Pictures are placed throughout the book as a reminder of the child's world and ways for adults to enter it. The reader may be surprised to see so many photographs showing children in a light-hearted fashion. These pictures illustrate how much time children spend with play and fantasy, no matter what their life circumstances or inner feelings may be. An active, playing child can still be a grieving child. Children escape and deny just as adults do. Yet their form for working through much of their grief is play.

I have chosen to use real life ancedotes to illustrate typical situations. Each story is followed by a section with practical ideas on how to help a child understand each situation and adjust to the change. Ways to prepare for grief, resources to use, and follow-up activities are included. This simplified but structured approach is beneficial in working with a wide range of circumstances. The basic ideas can be modified and expanded to fit new challenges that arise in the life of a child.

I chose the title, *Life and Loss: A Guide to Help Grieving Children*, for many reasons. While we need to recognize death as an important part of life, it is only one of many losses children experience. Whether over a broken toy, a broken leg, a broken home, or a broken heart, children grieve and mourn. Moving, divorce, and illness are issues interwoven into the threads of grief work that exist side by side with the death of a loved one (pet, friend, neighbor, sibling, parent, or grandparent). Additionally, in today's world, we must address the issues of violence, abuse, homicide, and suicide that also impact our children's everyday lives.

In the first chapter, the stage of understanding is set by providing loss and grief statistics leading into the twenty-first century. It explores the categories of childhood losses, emphasizing the loss of a future and protection for today's children. Suggestions on how to help are presented. The remaining chapters develop a deeper understanding of concepts that underlie Chapter 1.

The myths of loss and grief with which we, as caring adults, have been reared and then pass on to our children are explored in Chapter 2. We need to acknowledge these myths and replace them with facts.

The four psychological tasks of grief are explained in Chapter 3. Material is presented to provide an understanding of each task. Limiting clichés are replaced by more appropriate responses. The child's developmental understanding from birth to adolescence is viewed. Ways to commemorate are offered. The story of Star, a pet dog that has died, offers practical ideas for real life situations.

Identifying behaviors associated with grief and loss is the first step in actively working with children's needs. Chapter 4 discusses this and then presents grief resolution techniques that can

be used at home, in school, or on the playground, such as storytelling, letter writing, children's questions, drama, artwork, music, crafts, and other projective techniques that access and expand griefwork with children.

Chapter 5 is a special story that provides a needed answer to the questions of what to say when a child wants to say goodbye to a dying person. Through one mother's eyes, we are provided with a world of knowledge, and then we broaden her ideas

to include a general format for other loss and grief issues. Resources are offered for children who are living with dying. Ways to say goodbye at the memorial service and funeral home are also included.

Chapter 6 is especially for educators. It describes the challenges they and their students face daily. Guidelines for educational referrals and a children's loss inventory are included. Practical ways to use teachable moments in the classroom are described, as are resources especially for educators.

The idea of A Community Grief Team is developed in Chapter 7, "Where do we go from here?" Parent education, advocacy in the school system, child education, professional training, and multicultural considerations are explained, and a model of this team is presented.

Chapter 8 lists national resources that can be helpful to adults working with children. A general list of community resources for caregivers is included to help a community networking system. Children's grief camps and hotlines are included as important supports.

An exploration of materials is possible through Chapter 9, where annotations are included for books for adults and children, videos, manuals, CD-ROM, guides, and curricula. Valuable websites for families and professionals about loss and grief have also been included. Children's literature is divided into categories according to the loss issue. Age appropriateness is considered throughout.

This second edition of *Life and Loss,* as explained in the Preface, creates a framework for children's griefwork in the new millenium. Importantly, a vast amount of resources have been updated, some especially for educators and for those who work with children and their losses. Also included are websites, CD-ROM, and grief camps.

Grief resolution techniques have been added, demonstrating children's written work and artwork. The inclusion of two timely childhood losses—the loss of the protection of the adult world and the loss of a future—sets the stage for griefwork for today and tomorrow's children.

Denial, fear, shame, and lack of appropriate role models have shaped the lives of many adults. This often makes it difficult for us to relate to children with innocence, simplicity, and openness, especially in the sensitive areas of loss and grief. Yet, children are constantly being immersed in this ever-changing environment and need grown-ups to serve as role models for them. Parents, educators, and other caring professionals have the responsibility of helping these kids with their grief process. This guide has been written to serve as a role model. Through the use of photographs, children's work, anecodotes, simple techniques, and resources, we can tune in to the world of children. Hopefully, this book will help unlock the door of respect for the child's inner universe and allow us to enter into it with integrity.

> There appears to be so many grieving young people with so many difficult and diverse problems that we who live and work with them may often feel overwhelmed with the possible futility of impacting their lives. With the enormous amount of hurting children in today's and tomorrow's world, we may wonder if whatever strides we make can create a difference for the endless sea of grieving children.

It is my hope and prayer that we all begin today—joined together as co-creators of our own unique community grief team—by going back to our homes, our neighborhoods, our schools, our offices, our communities, and our worlds, with shared understanding and a renewed commitment: to help each and every child float through their ocean of grief on the unified minds and caring hearts of the adults and children that surround them.

Linda Goldman

CHAPTER 1
Children's Loss and Grief

DEATH • DRUGS • DIVORCE • ILLNESS
UNEMPLOYMENT • AIDS • ABUSE • POLLUTION
TERRORISM • HOMELESSNESS • NATURAL DISASTERS
BULLYING • MURDER • SUICIDE • VIOLENCE

That's What's the Matter with Kids Today

What's the Matter with Kids Today?

We asked ourselves, "What's the matter with kids today?" and discovered it is the answer, not the question. It is the answer because the very need to ask that question is an indication of adult denial. Adults have created this grief-filled world, and the children are confronted with its fear and chaos.

Donna O'Toole, a children's grief educator and author of *Growing Through Grief* (1989), warns that "Too often they [children] are the forgotten ones, lacking role models and assurances for a safe journey, they accumulate losses—attaching themselves to their memories," and literally can be left "frozen in time and buried alive in inner space" if they don't have the opportunity to work out their feelings.

We ask ourselves, "What's the matter with kids today? The answer is that the world is different than the one in which we grew up.

Today's children witness violence daily. A little boy asked his teacher who George Washington was. "He was our first President" was the reply. "Who shot him?" he asked, automatically assuming all presidents get shot.

In the 1992 movie, "Grand Canyon," a teenager involved in gang violence was asked by his uncle, "Why are you doing this? What will you do when you're 20?" "Are you kidding me? the teenager responded, "I'll be dead by 20."

TODAY'S FACTS ABOUT CHILDREN'S GRIEF

Today's children are confronted by a set of experiences and memories largely incomprehensible to us. The following statistics illustrate this point:

Death

Twelve percent of all childhood deaths (accidents, suicides, and murders) are caused by guns. Eleven children are killed every day.

Auto accidents are the leading cause of accidental deaths of children. Drownings are second.

In a school system of 6000 students, an average of four students die a year.

Twenty percent of today's children will have experienced the death of a parent by the end of high school.

Divorce

Over 6 million children are living in divorced families. One-third will lose contact with one parent.

Fifty percent of today's children will experience parental divorce by the end of high school.

Sexual Abuse

One out of three girls are sexually abused by age 18.
One out of seven boys are sexually abused by age 18.

Relocation

Today's children will have experienced an average of four moves per family by the end of high school.

Exposure to Violence

A child by age 14 will witnesses 18,000 deaths (usually violent murders) on T.V.

One in six children between the ages of 10 and 17 has seen or knows someone who has been shot.

Sources: Donna O'Toole, *Growing Through Grief* (1989); Alan Wolfelt, *Centerpiece Publication* (1992); S. Victor & Edith Lombardo, *Kids Grieve Too* (1986); Jerry Adler, *Kids Growing Up Scared* (1994).

The Washington Post reported on September 3, 1998, that ninth to twelfth grade students in Washington DC indicated their lives are filled with risky behaviors (See survey results below).

PERCENT OF TEENAGERS SAY THAT THEY HAVE:

- Carried a weapon in the past 30 days   32%
- Ridden in a car whose driver had been drinking   35%
- Taken five or more drinks within a couple of hours   18%
- Used marijuana   28%
- Had sexual intercourse   71%
- Had sexual intercourse with more than 3 people   38%
- Attempted suicide within the past 12 months   10%

What can we do for the children?

We can help the children by first helping ourselves. Our honesty in seeing and relaying loss and grief issues that run through our lives will indeed be the role model for our children. By networking with other caring adults and using the many resources available, we can minimize our fear and denial of loss and create an environment in which children know their own strength and power and can face and work through their pain.

❝ *Developing your psychological strength is just like developing physical abilities. The more you exercise, the stronger you become.* ❞

Harold Bloomfield and Leonard Felder,
Archilles Syndrome. (1986).
New York: Random House.

Childhood Loss

I have come to believe that all hurt and pain is based on tangible or intangible losses. From the loss of a child's tooth to the death of a parent, we grieve what we miss and want back—whether it be a mom, a pet, a toy, or our dignity and respect. Childhood losses can fall into one of the following categories (O'Toole, 1989 and Goldman, 1998):

- Relationships
- The Environment
- Skills/Ability
- Loss of Future/Protection of Adults
- External Objects
- Self
- Habits

LOSS OF RELATIONSHIPS

 Death of a parent, grandparent, sibling, friend, classmate, pet
Absence of teacher, parent, sibling, friend
Unavailability of parent due to alcoholism, drugs, imprisonment, divorce

The death of a pet can be a significant loss in a child's life. Consider the following two anecdotes:

Ellen, age 9, loved her dog very much. Buffy was her friend and companion. She fed him, brushed him, walked with him, and talked with him. During the school day, Buffy got hit by a car and died. A neighbor, out of kindness, took Buffy's body to the vet so that Ellen wouldn't have to see it. Ellen never got to say goodbye. "It's only a dog," her parents said. "We'll get you another one."

There was no other dog for Ellen. She loved Buffy and he was gone. Deeply mourning his loss for years to come, Ellen continued to carry this grief because she had no environment in which to mourn openly.

Sam loved his dog too. Sam played ball with Charlie every day after school. Charlie was a problem pet. Because Charlie was never completely housetrained or disciplined, Sam's parents made several unsuccessful attempts to sell Charlie or give him away. One day, Sam came home from school and his dog was gone. Sam's parents said they gave Charlie to a good home. Sam, questioned the truth of that explanation—no one had ever wanted to take Charlie before. The facts of Charlie's disappearance haunted Sam through his teenage years. Was Charlie killed? Was he abandoned? Was he hurt? Where did he go?

What Can We Do for the Child?

1. Tell children the truth about the pet's death or other events surrounding the pet's leaving.

2. Allow children to see the pet after it had died, if the body is relatively intact. It helps make death real.

3. Have a funeral and burial for the pet when possible. If pets are too large to bury, or a backyard is too small, a memorial service is an appropriate ritual. Let the children have a part in creating it.

4. Acknowledge children's memories and encourage them to talk about their pet.

5. Encourage children to express their feelings. Express your own.

6. Be aware of the child's guilty feelings that in some way the death or disappearance of the pet was his or her fault. (Why didn't I stay home from school that day? Why did I let my dog go outside?) Discuss ways the child was good to his or her pet. Discuss regrets too.

7. Use rituals to work through grief. Look at photos. Write down feelings and memories. Draw a picture for or of the pet. Save a special object (collar or ball) in a special place.

8. Have parents inform the child's school. Have educators let the child know they care. Use discussions as a teachable moment in school.

Network: Use a support system of people who understand the depth of grief involving pet loss (family, friends, veterinarians).

Call the Pet Loss Hot Line at (916) 752-4200 (Monday through Friday).

Resources:

Jim's Dog Muffin by Miriam Cohen (1994)

About Dying by Sarah Stein (1974)

When A Pet Dies by Fred Rogers (1988)

It Must Hurt A Lot by Doris Sanford (1985a)

LOSS OF EXTERNAL OBJECTS

 Loss of favorite toy or object (blanket, pacifier, teddy bear)
Loss through robbery or being misplaced (diary, special gift)

Losing things of value can be very difficult for children. Consider the following:

Nancy always traveled with Lizzie, her favorite stuffed koala bear. When Nancy visited Grandma, slept over at friends, or traveled with her family, Lizzie was the first thing Nancy packed. Her family's trip to San Francisco proved traumatic. After the first night in a fine hotel, Nancy and her parents went out to explore the city. Returning at bedtime they discovered Lizzie was gone. They searched and searched. Nancy cried and cried. "How can I sleep without Lizzie," she wept. "I want to go home."

What Can We Do for the Child?

1. Validate children's deep feelings for their personal property as a truly important companion.
2. Actively share in the search for the missing object.
3. Actively employ a self-help group. (For example, the hotel staff searched for Lizzie. Two days later Lizzie was found in the hotel's laundry room. A little cleaner, a little shrunken, and ever ready to be held and loved again.)

Resources:

A Bunch of Balloons by Dorothy Ferguson (1992)

The Fall of Freddie the Leaf by Leo Buscaglia (1982)

I Know I Made It Happen by Lynn Blackburn (1991)

LOSS IN THE ENVIRONMENT

 Fire, floods, hurricanes, and other natural disasters
Moving, changing school, changing family structure
Family separation

Family separation can be a painful grieving process for a young child. Whether it is leaving Mom to stay with a babysitter, a parent going on a trip, or a grandmother dying, the loss is real and important.

When my little boy Jonathan was five, I went away for six days. When I came back I asked him how it was for him when I was gone. He said, "Well, I got a little angry when people kept asking where you were, and Mom, what does 'unbearable' mean?" I answered, "Something really hard to take." He replied, "It was unbearable!"

What Can We Do for the Child?

1. Prepare children for the parent's departure. Whether a parent leaves for an hour, a day, a week, indefinitely, or forever, the child needs to know the facts. Open discussion decreases anxiety.

2. If the separation has an end date, make a calendar with the child that shows how long the parent will be away. Leave it in his or her room. The child can mark off the days.

3. Leave a picture of the parent by the child's bed.

4. Use a tape recorder for the child to talk to the parent or work out feelings about the parent leaving.

5. Leave the phone number of a caring adult who can support the child.

6. Inform the teacher about what has or will be happening at home.

Resources:

The Good Bye Book by Judith Viorst (1992)

About Change and Moving by Joy Berry (1990)

Please Come Home by Doris Sanford (1985b)

My Daddy Takes Care of Me by Patricia Quinlin (1987)

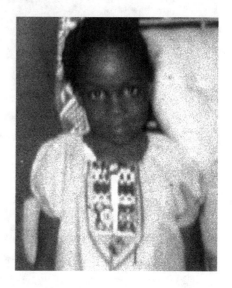

LOSS OF SELF

 Loss of physical part of the body: tooth, arm, eye
Loss of self-esteem: physical, sexual, emotional, or deprivational abuse

Behavioral symptoms of grief are not always fighting, crying, or other outward expressions. Children can withdraw, detach, or depersonalize life to escape issues of grief so painful that not feeling and not talking are the only ways to survive. Consider the following case of Mary:

Mary's dad had committed suicide when she was five. Never told the facts, she was informed that he died in an accident. Taken from her natural mother and not told why (although Mary later discovered that Mom was an alcoholic), Mary went to live with an aunt and uncle. Mary was extremely withdrawn in school. No one asked why. Her uncle sexually abused her from age five through nine. She became more and more withdrawn. Still no one asked why—not at school, not at church, not her friend's parents, not the community. At age nine, Mary began begging not to be left alone with her uncle. She was punished inappropriately and told that she was unappreciative.

Where were the adults, the advocates, the voices for the withdrawn children who carry the emotional pain of loss and grief that is heavy and filled with fear and abandonment? These children's silent cries scream to be heard by someone who can help. We need to open our ears to the quiet of the voiceless children. Let's hear their pain with our hearts.

Mary quietly withdrew, becoming shy and unapproachable. She seemed to internalize her problems of dealing with adults. When she bravely attempted to talk about her problems, they were denied by her adult world.

Mark, a 15-month-old, acted out his hurt in a different way to secure attention. Mark's Mom asked what she could do for her son, who was showing visable signs of distress after returning from visiting his dad. The couple had divorced, partially due to the husband's abusive nature. The child clung to his mom, cried a lot, had temper tantrums, and didn't want to be left alone. The court ruling had given the father two-day visitation rights, even though his abuse of his wife was on record. Mark's mom also said she noticed a bruise on the child and was angry about it. "I know my husband hits Mark but I don't know what to do about it."

 For adults trying to help children like Mary and Mark, knowing the signs of abuse is the first step in confronting their abusive situations, whether the abuse is physical, sexual, or by neglect.

What Can We Do for the Children?

To help children who are being abused, we must first know and understand the signs of abused children and abusive parents.

Signs of Abuse in Children

With the help of Nancy Eike, director of North West Child Protective Network of the Omni Youth Service, I have adapted the following indicators of abuse in children. It is essential for parents, teachers, counselors, clergy, and pediatricians to watch for internal (verbal) or external (physical) signs. If more than one of the following signs are present, you need to report the suspected findings to the proper authorities. You should suspect abuse if a child:

- is habitually away from school and constantly late
- arrives at school very early and leaves very late because he or she does not want to go home
- is compliant, shy, withdrawn, passive, or uncommunicative
- is nervous, hyperactive, aggressive, disruptive, or destructive
- has an unexplained injury—a patch of hair missing, a burn, a limp, or bruises
- has an inappropriate number of unexplained injuries, such as bruises on his or her arms or legs over a period of time
- exhibits an injury that is not adequately explained
- complains about numerous beatings
- complains about the mother's boyfriend "doing things" when the mother is not home
- has difficulty going to the bathroom
- is inadequately dressed for inclement weather
- wears a long sleeved blouse or shirt during the summer (may cover bruises on the arms)
- has clothing that is soiled, tattered, or too small
- is dirty, smells, or has bad teeth, hair falling out, or lice
- is thin, emaciated, and constantly tired, showing evidence of malnutrition and dehydration
- is usually fearful of other children and adults
- has been given inappropriate food, drink, or drugs
- talks about someone touching his or her private parts

Signs of Abusive Parents

Child abuse should be suspected and reported by any caring adult if the parents have more than one of the following:

- little concern for their child's problems
- no responses to the teacher's inquiries and absences from parent's night or private teacher conferences
- spent an unusual amount of time seeking health care for the child
- inadequate explanations for their child's injury
- different explanations for the same injury
- attributed the cause of an injury to the child or a third party
- reluctance to share information about the child
- inappropriate responses to the seriousness of the problem
- tendency to disappear
- current alcohol or drug use issues
- no friends, relatives, or neighbors to turn to in times of crisis
- have unrealistic expectations for the child
- very strict discipline practices
- abuse, neglect, or deprivation in their past
- taken the child to different doctors, clinics, or hospitals for past injuries (possibly trying to cover up the fact of repeated injuries);
- signs of loss of control or a fear of losing control
- antagonistic and hostile behaviors when talking about the child's health problems

Nancy Eike emphasizes that "these clues can help adults make an informed decision about reporting." Educators in particular are only required to report *suspected* abuse to the proper authorities. Investigating is the responsibility of the authorities. Parents can obtain supporting documentation from other official caregiving settings. No one needs to disclose his or her name when reporting suspected abuse to their state's Children's Protective Services. These agencies must act within 24 to 48 hours. They may decide not to separate the child from the family. However, each report will add strength to the next one made about the same abuse case.

What Can We Do for the Child?

For children under 3, their primary needs are met by physical comforting, such as hugging, holding, and permitting appropriate regression. Caregiving adults who abuse their children need guidance in working with their anger so that they become freer to love their children.

Doris Sanford is the author of *I Can't Talk About It*, an excellent book for children on sexual abuse. She stresses it is important to:

1. encourage *no* self blame,
2. encourage repetition of telling the story,
3. assure total belief of the abuse,
4. maintain privacy,
5. control your anger about the abuse,
6. offer protection,
7. remember that sometimes there are no visible signs of abuse, and
8. acknowledge you feel bad about the abuse.

> **"** *There is no place so potentially violent as home. It is sometimes a place of special betrayal because the child's guard is down. If you are abusing a child, please accept help. If you are being abused, tell someone and keep telling until you get the help you need.* **"**

Doris Sanford, I Can't Talk About It. (1986).
Portland, OR: Quesatar Publications, Multnomah Press.

Resources:

Helping Your Child Recover from Sexual Abuse by Karen Adams and Jennifer Fay (1992)

I Can't Talk About It by Doris Sanford (1986)

Something Is Wrong in My House by Diane Davis Childhood (1984)

LOSS RELATED TO SKILLS AND ABILITIES

 Held back in school
Not chosen for team sports
Overweight, injured, illness, physical disability
Dyslexia, ADHD, other developmental differences

In my first year of teaching, I was given a second grade class of 22 repeaters. We were placed in a trailer away from the school. Some of the children were labeled slow learners, others were on medication for ADHD (Attention Deficit Hyperactivity Disorder), still others just seemed to be neglected at home. The children began school with the shame and stigma of failing second grade individually and as a group. The humiliation extended to their physical isolation in the trailer. I looked at their faces the first day of class and saw a lack of joy and an aura of poor self-esteem. They knew they were different and felt the despair of their perceived lack of achievement.

What Can We Do for the Child?

1. Recognize the facts about the child's school placement.

2. Allow children opportunities to discuss their retention or loss openly.

3. Incorporate the children's thoughts and feelings into creative writing and language experience.

4. Accept the children for where they are academically, athletically, or physically by using projects and tasks geared to their level of ability and comfort. See growth as individually progressing, and not just as standardized grade level comparisons of where children should be.

5. Create a project where the children can shine. For example, since the repeating second graders are a year older than the other second grade class, use the maturity in a creative way (plays, murals, school service projects).

6. Use every opportunity to encourage self-esteem. The following poem is a creative way (with a little humor) to bring home the point for adults and children that despite outward differences, we're all alike inside.

No Difference

Small as a peanut,
Big as a giant,
We're all the same size
When we turn off the light.

Rich as a sultan,
Poor as a mite,
We're all worth the same
When we turn off the light.

Red, black, or orange,
Yellow or white,
We all look the same
When we turn off the light.

So maybe the way
To make everything right
Is for someone to just reach out
And turn off the light!

Source: *Where The Sidewalk Ends* by Shel Silverstein (1974). HarperCollins Publishers. Reprinted by permission.

LOSS RELATED TO HABITS

Sucking thumb, biting fingernails, twirling hair
Change in eating patterns or daily routines
Beginning or ending school

A bus accident on the way to school can certainly change the routine of the day for the children involved. This happened to a group of 25 elementary school children.

Timmy was the only first grader among them. The bus swerved to avoid a truck and was thrown over on its side. Miraculously, no one was severely was severely hurt. The children waited for the police, were taken to the hospital in ambulances, and the parents were notified. The accident was a disturbing disruption to the school routine. Some kids were emotionally shaken. One child fainted. Other kids were bruised and cut. Timmy had a few scrapes on his face. He raced to his mom when she entered the hospital, hugged her tightly, and insisted in a frightened voice, "I'm never riding the bus again, and you can't make me!"

What Can We Do for the Child?

1. Bring children together to discuss feelings about their bus accident experience. Listen and echo back feelings.

2. Allow each child the time and space to retell his or her version of the story. This helps to see where support or clarification is needed.

3. Let each child mark on a diagram of the bus where he or she was and tell what he or she did.

4. Recognize any injuries that the children sustained.

5. Discuss guilt that some children may feel if they were one of the ones not injured.

6. Identify the fears for future bus rides. Reassure that everything has been done to ensure safety.

7. Bring the entire school together for an assembly. Discuss what an accident is and the facts surrounding the bus accident. Allow all children time for questions. This will respond to the needs of the school children who were not on the bus.

8. Inform parents of all the children in the school. Send home the facts of the accident and how it has been handled with their children.

9. Listen, and respond with care, because children often refer to their scary experience in their talk or play for many months after the accident. To do so is normal and healthy.

10. Have parents and teachers reassure children: it was an accident, no one was seriously hurt, and we are all O.K.

 Human beings and especially children can survive very frightening experiences.

Network:
1. Set up a telephone network for the kids who were on the bus to call each other and share their feelings.

2. Set up a time during school where these kids who were in the accident can continue to share their feelings.

Resources:

Alexander and the Terrible Horrible No Good Very Bad Day by Judith Viorst (1972)

Don't Pop Your Cork on Monday by Adolph Moser (1988)

About Traumatic Experiences by Joy Berry (1990)

LOSS OF THE PROTECTION OF THE ADULT WORLD: LOSS OF A FUTURE

Loss of role models
Fears of school as a dangerous place
Lack of motivation for school work
Choice of violence as a way of solving problems

Amanda was a sixth grade student in an inner city school system. Her dad was murdered outside of her home, her mom is addicted to crack cocaine, and her brother committed suicide. Amanda was often sent to the office for using bad language, cutting school, and fighting. Her English teacher sent her once again to the vice principal, Mr. Henry, because she refused to complete her assignment "What I want to do when I grow up." Mr. Henry began questioning Amanda:

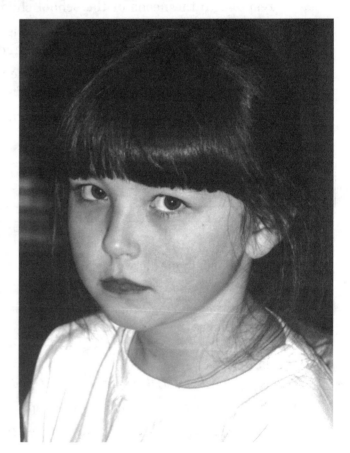

"Why," he asked, "do you refuse to do your homework?"

"Why should I?" Amanda shouted and banged her fist on the table.

"I won't live to be in seventh grade!"

Mr. Henry asked her to write her theme about that.

Amanda is one of millions of children that live every day surrounded by violence and abuse with no outlet to share it or voice to speak of it. Too many of today's traumatized, grief-stricken children see no future and are unable to visualize themselves growing into adulthood. Seeing no future, it is unlikely that the Amanda's of today's world will be motivated to do assignments for tomorrow when tomorrow may not exist for them. Boys and girls that may not directly experience these issues are inundated by the media visually and auditorally that these kinds of things could happen to them, creating and compounding unwarranted fears of lack of protection and future safety for all of them.

What Can We Do for the Child?

1. Encourage police, coaches, big brothers, big sisters, and senior citizens to volunteer as mentors and role models for the grieving child.

2. Create awareness of neighborhood watch programs and buddy systems to provide protection for children before and after school.

3. Maintain programs, assemblies, and school policies on bullying, violence, and weapons in school.

4. Parents and school personnel can create a time each day for children to voice their fears and concerns about the violence and trauma that may surround their life or their vicarious fears through media imput.

5. Provide class meetings that allow kids to safely discuss fears.

6. Use life issues social studies and guidance curriculums in the school system that are geared to working with children who have experienced violence, abuse, death, and other trauma.

Resources:

The No-Bullying Curriculum by James Bitney and James and Beverly Title (1996)

Succeeding with Multiple Intelligences by Sally Boggeman, Tom Hoerr, and Christine Wallach (Eds.) (1996).

Reactions by Alison Salloum (1998)

Children Are Survivors Too by Kathleen Auk (1995)

C H A P T E R   2

Myths of Grief

- "YOU'LL GET OVER IT."
- "CRYING WON'T HELP."
- "BE STRONG FOR YOUR MOM."
- "IT'S TIME TO MOVE ON."
- "YOU'RE TOO YOUNG TO UNDERSTAND."

Myths About Loss and Grief

This chapter discusses the following 10 myths.

1. Grief and mourning are the same experience.
2. Adults can instantly give explanations to children about death and spirituality.
3. The experience of grief and mourning has orderly stages.
4. The grief of adults does not impact on the bereaved child.
5. Adults should avoid topics that cause a child to cry.
6. An active, playing child is not a grieving child.
7. Infants and toddlers are too young to grieve.
8. Parents, educators, and clergy are always prepared and qualified to give explanations and clarifications regarding loss and grief.
9. Children need to "get over" their grief and move on.
10. Children are better off not attending funerals.

 If a child is old enough to love, he or she is old enough to grieve.

Source: adapted from Alan Wolfelt, author of *Helping Children Cope with Grief*, 1983.

We ask ourselves, "What's the matter with kids today?" and we answer, "They are being reared on the same myths of grief on which we were reared when we were young."

MYTH: GRIEF, BEREAVEMENT, AND MOURNING ARE THE SAME

Grief is defined as a normal, internalized reaction to the loss of a person, thing, or idea. It is our emotional response to loss.

Bereavement is the state of having lost something, whether it be significant others, significant things, or our sense of self. This state can range from the death of a parent, the destruction of a home, to the loss of dreams, dignity, and self-respect.

Mourning means taking the internal experience of grief and expressing it outside of ourselves. It is the cultural expression of grief, as seen in traditional or creative rituals. Traditional rituals refer to ones that are sanctioned culturally, such as funerals. Creative rituals can be writing a letter to the deceased and then destroying it. Rituals are the behaviors we use to do grief work.

The story of Nicholas illustrates how a child's grief and mourning greatly affects his life.

His mourning became a burden to the school. He began acting out in school, fighting with friends, using bad language, writing graffiti wherever he could, failing school work, and complaining of stomachaches. The private school that Nicholas attended had little tolerance for his behaviors and asked him to leave, even though he had been there from kindergarten until eighth grade.

Many times, bereaved children mourn through behaviors rather than words. His parents were getting divorced, and the situation was further compounded by his school abandoning him. Nicholas clearly exhibited behaviors to watch for in grieving children. These include anxiety, hostility towards others, and bodily distress. Had the educators in his school looked at his behaviors in a different way, the system may not have failed. Nicholas was an unrecognized mourner. He was grieving but was not given the appropriate conditions to mourn in order to work out his feelings of loss.

In yesterday's world, Nicholas' acting out in school might have been the worst that could have happened. In today's world, another Nicholas may have just as easily brought a loaded pistol and shot a teacher or classmate, or turned to escapism through drugs or even suicide.

MYTH: ADULTS CAN INSTANTLY GIVE EXPLANATIONS TO CHILDREN ABOUT DEATH AND SPIRITUALITY

It's OK to admit we don't know all the answers—and not feel guilty that we can't define God in heaven or what happens after death. Life and death can be mysteries. A good example to illustrate to young children that sometimes things are part of a larger picture than we can see and understand is the book, *Look Again,* by Tana Hoban (1971). Using smaller parts of a larger photograph, children see there is a much larger picture than they possibly could have imagined.

MYTH: GRIEF AND MOURNING HAVE ORDERLY STAGES

The concept of stages of grief often is misunderstood to be progressive and alike for everyone in every way. Grief work is unique to every adult and every child. Each person approaches it in his or her own way and at his or her own pace.

	No two people are alike, and neither is their grief.

An attitude that allows the child to be the true expert on his or her feelings is one that says, "Teach me about your grief and I will be with you." We must remind ourselves not to prescribe how children should grieve and mourn, but allow them to teach us where they are in the process.

Two sons had very different reactions to their mother's cancer, chemotherapy, and loss of hair. The oldest, a preadolescent, was very embarrassed and refused to share his feelings. When he first saw his mom in a wig, he threw a towel over his head and ran out of the room. The youngest boy, a six-year-old, talked about his feelings a lot. Yet, he still had many nightmares. His teacher later shared that he had been writing a story in an ongoing journal every month about his baby-sitter who was very sick and eventually died.

We can ask ourselves how we would treat these children by knowing their age level and what they told us about their process.

MYTH: THE GRIEF OF ADULTS DOES NOT IMPACT THE BEREAVED CHILD

Parents, teachers, and adult friends are significant models for children. How adults mourn sets an example for surrounding children. If adults deny their grief, the children probably will do the same. If adults allow themselves to be sad or angry, it gives permission for the children to be sad or angry. Often adults try to hide their feelings from kids, falsely believing it is in the children's best interest. The guilt that a child may feel after someone he or she loves has left (as in divorce or moving) or died (due to an accident or illness) can be acknowledged and released if adult modeling allows for expression of feelings.

 By allowing ourselves to mourn, we help the bereaved child to mourn.

Another aspect of adult mourning affecting children is the absence of the grieving parent emotionally and perhaps physically as well. This is a secondary loss for kids. Many times, the caregiving parent is so distraught that he or she too is missing for the child for a period of time. It's a good idea to provide kids with a caring adult who can be a support system until the grieving parent has worked out some of his or her pain.

MYTH: ADULTS SHOULD AVOID TOPICS THAT CAUSE A CHILD TO CRY

Jeff, a second grader, began acting out in school. He began being very demanding of his friends, requiring extreme loyalty from them, needing to be boss at all times, and ultimately rejecting their friendship. His teacher talked to him several times about friendship and what he needed to do to be a good friend. After many conversations, Jeff burst into tears. "Well, all my friends have left me," he sobbed. Crying was Jeff's way of relieving his tension and communicating his hurt and need to be comforted. It turned out that his four best friends had left his school at the end of first grade. He was mourning their loss and working out his feelings of abandonment.

His teacher did many good things to help Jeff heal. She trusted her instincts and initiated a discussion with Jeff, even though he had not brought it up himself. She saw his behaviors as a sign of grief, rather than a threat. She gave his loss validity and encouraged classmates to be a new support system for him.

Jeff's teacher led Jeff to realize he had a lot of good memories with his old friends and still could be with them even though they weren't at school. Jeff called his old friends and reestablished their relationship for after school. He began to be less demanding of school friends. Jeff's teacher did not continue the myth that children need to be brave. Rather, she consciously did not avoid the painful topic that caused him to cry and helped Jeff get in touch with and ultimately overcome his pain.

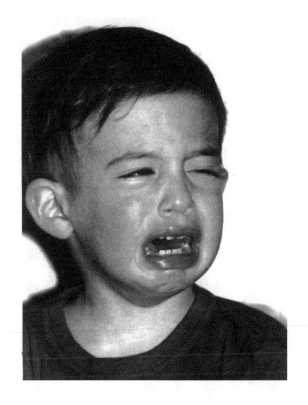

Jim was sad too. His dad was in intensive care after his heart attack. He was told, "You need to be strong for your mom," "Tears won't make him well," and "He wouldn't want you to cry."

Unfortunately, many adults associate tears of grief with personal weakness, especially for males.

Crying children can make adults feel helpless. Out of a wish to protect children (and themselves), well-meaning adults often directly inhibit tears.

> **We, as caring adults, can acknowledge the sadness a child feels if he or she fails a test, repeats a school year, or strikes out in a baseball game. We, as caring adults, can also acknowledge the sadness if the class is doing a Father's Day project and a child's dad is in the hospital, out of work, in jail, or has died. In this way, the child learns it is OK to feel his feelings.**

MYTH: AN ACTIVE PLAYING CHILD IS NOT A GRIEVING CHILD

Don't expect children to mourn in the same way you do. Some may cry or say they are sad, some may appear not to be feeling anything, and others may show anger and hurt. All of these reactions need to be accepted.

Remember, a child can work out feelings best through play. What may appear to be a frivolous play activity to us may well be an important part of the child's mourning process.

Allison's best friend had moved away. She was missing her. A sensitive teacher gave her a toy telephone and suggested she call her. Allison began calling her on the play phone at school, telling her how much she missed her and asking when she was coming back? She was given an opportunity through play to work out her feelings.

MYTH: INFANTS AND TODDLERS ARE TOO YOUNG TO GRIEVE

A dad told his boss at work, after the death of his oldest son, that he wouldn't explain anything to his two-year-old daughter because she was too young to understand.

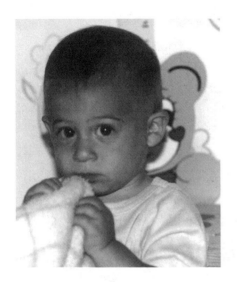

Alan Wolfelt, noted clinical thanaltologist and director of the Center of The Center For Loss and Life Transition, emphasizes that "any child who is old enough to love is old enough to mourn." (*Helping Children Cope with Grief*, 1983). Certainly toddlers and infants are capable of giving and receiving love, yet we often hear they are too young to understand.

Ernie was dying. Diagnosed with a terminal pulmonary disease, he and his young wife bravely and determinedly decided to have a child and to live to see him or her be born. With love and conviction, they accomplished their goals. Their son, Eli, was the joy of each of the precious days Ernie had left on earth. When Eli was two and a half months old, his dad died. A light went out in Eli's new life.

Fourteen months later, Eli and his Mom were taking a walk and spotted a man that remarkably resembled Eli's dad. Racing to the stranger, Eli wrapped his arms and legs around the man, clung to him with every ounce of Eli's little being, and refused to let go. His mom had to drag him away sobbing.

At sixteen months, Eli was mourning the death and the memories of his dad. Becoming noticeably sad after this experience, Eli began having difficulty sleeping and eating. His mom decided to be open with him in talking and sharing feelings. Intuitively, she knew a toddler was old enough to mourn, for he had certainly been old enough to love. She invited him to help create a photo album of dad and times shared together.

This album became one of the great treasures of Eli's childhood. He carried his book of photos with him constantly, literally holding his dad's love in his arms. A tangible bridge of memories had been created between Eli and his dad—a bridge of memories to last a lifetime.

MYTH: PARENTS, EDUCATORS, AND CLERGY ALWAYS ARE PREPARED AND QUALIFIED TO GIVE EXPLANATIONS AND CLARIFICATIONS REGARDING LOSS AND GRIEF

No one has all the answers, not even parents, teachers, counselors, or clergy.

When our baby Jennifer died, my husband and I knew no guidelines to help us through such a tragedy. We turned to a rabbi for help. "Do we have a funeral?" "How do we bury her?" "What can we do for her?" "Don't worry," he said. "In the Jewish religion, stillborn babies are not considered a life." We had just seen her, held her, gone through two days of labor with her, and nine months of pregnancy. We knew she was a life. We sought counsel within ourselves and found the right answers for us.

I sat across the table from a pastoral counselor at a meeting on how to talk to children about death. The counselor was worried about a mother who insisted she had four children although one had died. The counselor wondered how she could help the mother to see she was going too far by insisting she had four children. From the counselor's point of view, the mother clearly had three children. The counselor felt that this mother's child was dead and that she needed to cope with reality.

But who's reality? The mother's or the counselor's? Clearly this rabbi and this pastoral counselor never had a child die. They would know, "Once a mom, always a mom" though all time and space.

Susan Trout, Director of the Institute for the Advancement of Service and author of *To See Differently* (1990), gave me a precious gift by referring to Jennifer as "your daughter." It was the first time that any one had verbally acknowledged that I indeed had had a real daughter who died. Children need this validation, too, if a sibling dies—whether it be a preschooler, toddler, stillborn, or miscarriage. By referring to this death as "your sister" or "your brother," the child can more easily become in touch with all the powerful feelings that those words evoke.

MYTH: CHILDREN NEED TO "GET OVER" THEIR GRIEF AND MOVE ON

Children and adults are often told that they "should be over it by now—it's been almost a year." Adults who believe this myth deny children the patience to live with and to work with their grief.

Danny's teacher responded to the death of Danny's mom by telling him, "You have to forget about this and go on." Danny said he felt like killing his teacher! The last thing Danny wanted to do was to forget his mom. He needs to remember her in a positive way to take her with him on his journey through life.

Jonathan woke up one morning and decided to bring in a picture of his pet cat, Susie, for show-and-tell. She had died a year ago. When he came home from school that day he asked if he could see where she was buried. This was a healthy request, moving him towards healing. Both examples illustrate that coping with loss is ongoing.

Adults and kids often equate getting over grief with forgetting the person, without realizing that their pain is what connects them to their loss. We need to find alternative ways that connect them to the lost person or event, diffuse the pain, and transform it into a positive experience.

MYTH: CHILDREN ARE BETTER OFF NOT ATTENDING FUNERALS

Not allowing children to attend funerals creates an environment of denial that does not allow them to actively participate in the grieving process. The funeral provides a structure for the child to see how people comfort each other openly, mourn a loved one, and honor his or her life. Children learn the ways we say goodbye to the remains of the person who died and how we show respect for the deceased.

Chad's dad, Ray, drowned at age 31. Chad was seven. Chad's grandfather told Chad of his dad's death, and they cried together for a very long time. Ray's body was found after several days of being in the water, necessitating a closed casket funeral.

The family, including Chad, worked together to select meaningful items to be placed in the casket. A picture of Chad, a letter from Ray's mom, and some other items were chosen. Chad was made an important part of the funeral process and so the funeral process became an important part of him.

During the ceremony, Chad leaned over to his grandfather and whispered, "Granddad, I'm using my imagination right now and pretending I'm reaching inside the coffin and hugging Dad." He needed to say goodbye and created a way to do so.

> **Children assuredly follow their hearts to find their own unique ways to work through grief. Being present at the funeral, placing personal mementos in the coffin, and practicing in the ceremony are very concrete ways children can contribute to the process of saying good bye.**

My son Jonathan, age six, attended his first funeral when my sister's mother-in-law died. Jonathan said he wanted to go to the funeral, and he did. When the family was viewing the body, he wanted to look too. A slight panic ran through me as all of my training and knowledge said "yes," while I heard my mother's voice say, "no, go sit in the other room, Jonathan." The funeral director walked over to me and quietly said, "I didn't want to interfere, but I feel kids imagine far more and far worse if they aren't allowed to look at the body." Gratefully, I agreed. Jonathan walked over, viewed the body, and was quite satisfied. Surprisingly, my mother easily adjusted to the change of circumstance. Relaying the story to a friend, I was told that her son had chosen not to see the body of his grandmother and continually asks questions like, "Was Grandma's body bleeding or bruised or broken?"

We often shield children from the funeral experience because we think it is too difficult. It is difficult. By being allowed to choose to participate in a funeral of someone to whom he was not deeply emotionally attached, Jonathan was freer to incorporate the event and become prepared for future funerals of more closely connected loved ones. He came to see death as an open part of life.

These myths are barriers to the grieving process. They disguise our own vulnerability and feelings of helplessness, and perpetuate a world of denial.

We need a new way of looking at a universal issue of grief. We need to educate ourselves and our communities to distinguish between fact and fiction so that our children can too.

C H A P T E R   3

Four Psychological Tasks
of Grief Work

- UNDERSTANDING
  - GRIEVING
- COMMEMORATING
  - GOING ON

" *There are two choices when a loved one dies—to live in grief, remorse, and guilt covered thinly by a facade; or to face those feelings, work them through, and emerge with an acceptance of death and a commitment to living.* "

Edith Mize, R.N.
in Elisabeth Kubler Ross'
Death: The Final Stage of Growth (1975).

Children Work Through Grief: Four Psychological Tasks

Sandra Fox, past director of the Boston "Good Grief" program, cites four tasks children need to work through in order to grow. These tasks occur in every age level and for every type of loss. The four tasks are

- UNDERSTANDING

- GRIEVING

- COMMEMORATING

- GOING ON

UNDERSTANDING

Understanding is the first psychological task. Children need to make sense out of death. We define death as when the body stops working. Then each family can explain death in its own way. Dr. Fox suggested these possibilities: "In our family, we believe that when a person's body stops working, he dies, but we believe his soul or spirit lives on in heaven with God" or "but we believe he lives on in some form of plant or animal life."

We can explain unexpected deaths by reminding kids that "Most people live to be very, very old, but once in a while an accident, illness, or injury is so bad that doctors and hospitals can't help, and a person's body stops working."

We need to remember that children's understanding of death changes as they develop. Let's remember that kids perceive death differently at various childhood stages, and that their perceptions are a predictable influence of grief.

Understanding Effected by Magical Thinking

Magical thinking is a predictable interference with children's grief. Children feel responsible for what happens in the world around them. When a six-year-old screams at her brother, "I hate you! I wish you were dead!" and these become the last words spoken to her brother who died in a drowning accident the following morning, magical thinking can assuredly make her feel she caused this death. She may live with overwhelming guilt for many years to come.

Five-year-old Sam announced he had "killed [his] Mother." His mother died of cancer. Yet, Sam had always heard that "junk food could kill you," and he had given her soda the day before she died. The family did not talk to him about cancer, believing it was too terrible to talk about. As an adult, Sam still believes at some deep emotional level that he is in someway responsible for killing his mother.

The movie "Home Alone" is a wonderful fantasy illustrating how powerful children's magical thinking is. The boy in the film was angry and frustrated with his family and went to bed wishing they would all disappear. He woke up in an empty house and was sure he had orchestrated their disappearance, even though they really had forgotten to take him on the family vacation.

Understanding Blocked by Common Clichés

Common clichés can hurt the grief process. Mandy's grandfather died. Her mom thinks, "I'll just tell her he's gone to heaven and that will take care of it." Mandy wonders, "If grandpa is in heaven, why did they put him in the ground?" or "Can I go to heaven too?"

We need to give honest answers to questions about death, using simple and direct language. Facts need to be presented accurately. Children will find them out in time. Telling children the truth will create an atmosphere of trust and confidence. Remember, children often take and believe what we say literally.

ALBERT LOST HIS MOTHER

- He did! Where? How? Did he look for her? How could he lose her? She was so tall! replied a panicked little voice.
- Children may fear the literal loss of their parents.
- **It is better to say,** Albert's mother died. He will miss her a lot.

DAD WENT ON A LONG TRIP

- Why didn't he say goodbye? Where did he go? his little daughter asked.
- Children may become afraid of anyone or themselves going on a trip.
- They may fear their parents leaving for work or generalize to just feeling abandoned.
- **It is better to say,** Dad died in a drowning accident. We all feel so sad, but we will get through it together.

IT IS GOD'S WILL (OR "GOD TOOK HIM BECAUSE HE IS SO GOOD" OR "HE'S IN HEAVEN WITH THE ANGELS.")

- Why doesn't God take me? I'm good, or I'll have to be bad so that God won't take me, thinks a little boy.
- A child may develop a fear of God or a fear of love.
- **It is better to say,** Grandpa died last night. We will think about him a lot. We can remember all of the wonderful things we did with him.

GRANDMA IS WATCHING YOU IN HEAVEN (SO YOU BETTER BE GOOD)

- The child thinks, What happens if I'm bad?
- Children can have paranoid feelings, become afraid of making mistakes, and feel guilty and stuck in any "bad" behaviors.
- **It is better to say,** Grandma was very, very old and died. Her love for us will live on in our memories.

MAX (THE CAT) WENT TO SLEEP LAST NIGHT (HE'S IN KITTY HEAVEN)

- Will I die when I go to sleep tonight? the child wonders.
- Children may develop a fear of sleep or darkness that could result in sleeplessness and nightmares.
- **It is better to say,** Max was very, very sick and the sickness made him die. No one really knows if he went to heaven. Some people believe that he does, and some people don't.

Understanding Children's Developmental Stages

A child's understanding of death changes as he or she develops. Knowing how children perceive death at different developmental stages of childhood is important so that we can then work with predictable and appropriate responses.

AGE: 0–2

PIAGET'S STAGE OF DEVELOPMENT: SENSORIMOTOR

Child Concept of Death: "All Gone"

- "Out of sight, out of mind" appears to be the infant's perception. If the young infant cannot see something, it does not exist.
- Peekaboo or hide-and-seek are games that after six months help develop the concept that things and people exist even if we can't see them.

AGE: 2–7

PIAGET' STAGE OF DEVELOPMENT: PREOPERATIONAL

Child's Concept of Death: Magical, Egocentric, and Causal

- Child thinks death is temporary and partial.
- Preschoolers see death as reversable, a journey from which there is a return.
- A child conceives the possibility of reviving the dead person by giving hot food or keeping the body warm.
- The child believes some functions continue, like feeling and thinking.
- Children may see dead people as living in a box underground, connected to other boxes by tunnels, or on a cloud in a place called heaven. Jonathan, a six-year-old, explained that "Heaven is a place way deep underground, deeper than anyone has ever gone, deeper than bulldozers go. Your body disintegrates and goes there."

- The child thinks his or her own thoughts or actions could cause death. The child feels guilt and fear of retribution for perceived bad things done or angry thoughts. A child tells mom she hates her and wishes she was dead. Mom is killed in an accident the next day. The child's magical thinking convinces the child that she caused her mother's death.
- The child thinks death is like sleep. This creates a fear of sleep and darkness, and the child needs to be reassured.
- The child gives inaccurate estimates of an average life span. The child thinks that "people live for 150 years."

AGE: 7–12

PIAGET'S STAGE OF DEVELOPMENT: CONCRETE OPERATIONS

Child's Concept of Death: Curious and Realistic

- Children are curious and inquisitive about birth, death, and sex differences . They are very interested in details of death.
- Children begin to internalize the universality and permanence of death. They can conceptualize that all body functions stop.
- Dead people can't breathe, move, hear, or see. Children are aware of a death vocabulary. They can express logical thoughts and fears about death.
- Children can comprehend thoughts of a belief in an afterlife.
- Children can accurately estimate how long people live.
- Children think of death's occurence in specific observable concrete terms. They may ask, "What are the reasons people die?" (War, poison, floods, car accidents, plane crashes, murders, etc.)
- Children still basically believe that the very old, the severely handicapped, and the extremely awkward people are the ones who die.

AGE 13 AND UP:

PIAGET'S STAGE OF DEVELOPMENT: FORMAL OPERATIONS, IMPLICATIONS, AND LOGIC

Adolescent's Concept of Death: Self-Absorbed

- Adolescents understand mortality and death as a natural process.
- They often have a difficult time with death because they are absorbed with shaping their own lives. Death seems remote and something they can't control.
- The denial of their own death is strong. They usually feel death is caused by old age or serious illness.
- Adolescents are more comfortable talking about death with peers than with adults.

Julie and Lila are two young girls who chose to use writing as a way to work out their feelings. Julie, a five-year-old, had a cousin Mary who had died. Julie kept dictating letters to her cousin and asking her mother to mail them. She didn't understand that death was not reversible.

Ten-year-old Lila, mourning her Uncle Bryan's death, had a different issue. Rather that writing to Bryan, she wrote about Bryan in private poetry she kept hidden in her room. She understood only too well how final death was but felt ashamed to share it.

At age five, Julie had no problem being open about her feelings, but she didn't really understand the nature of death. By age ten, Lila did understand what death was about, but she was uncomfortable being open about her feelings.

Uncle Bryan
is a Flower Blooming

by Lila Feikin (3/92)

When he comes light-jogging
  into my arms . . . he delights me.
Like a child getting his own pet,
  And I still love him.
He always was playing sports
  And he puts a smile on my face.

When he comes light walking
  into my heart
He opens his arms to me
Like vines wrapping around a tree
  . . . and I love him.

Even though he is gone
Uncle Byran is a flower
  blooming
. . . that fills me with joy.

GRIEVING

Grieving is the second psychological task for bereaved children and adolescents. Anger as well as death must be dealt with, and many times anger is less acceptable to parents, schools, and communities. Children's grief is an ongoing process, often continuing through adolescence.

ᴳᴳ *When someone you love dies, you have a feeling of numbness; a yearning; and a protest. You have lost part of yourself; you feel disorganized; and you do much crying. You're restless, and you may feel guilty. Perhaps you could have helped the one who died but you did not know how. You are angry because the person died, and you are angry at the world. You feel so alone, and loneliness is one of the biggest problems of grief.* **ᵞᵞ**

Edith Mize, R.N.
In Elisabeth Kubler-Ross' *DEATH: The Final Stage Of Growth*

Phases of Grief

Phases of grief can resurface at any time. A number of grief educators have suggested that grief can be seen as occurring in four phases. They are

- Shock and Disbelief
- Searching and Yearning
- Disorganization and Despair
- Rebuilding and Healing

   Source: Carol and David Eberling, *When Grief Comes to School,* 1991.

These are not rigid stages, but interchangeable and continuous processes.

We can see how they change through Bobby's story. Bobby's brother died when he was eight years old. His **shock** and **disbelief** began. He was very confused. He couldn't understand how his brother could be in the hospital, in the ground, in the funeral home, in heaven, and living in his memory all within the same week. He then began to **search** for meaning in a world that made no sense. Years later, at age 12, he began acting out at middle school, concerning his teachers and parents. He had been looking back on his brother's death with **despair**, believing his parents had let his brother die and would probably let Bobby die too.

A new phase of grief work began—**rebuilding** and **healing**. Bobby was reassured that everything had been done for his brother and would be done for Bobby, if needed. He discovered he had done much for his brother by holding him and sharing toys. Bobby's giving had really made a difference that no one could take away.

Bobby had learned to feel pain, be out of control, and gain mastery over his feelings. He began using a punching bag to work out some of his anger and choosing times to be alone when he was frustrated. Bobby's family had communicated clearly when his brother died, yet still misconceptions arose at a different stage of grief.

 We cannot expect to explain the loss instantly, and a child cannot learn it instantly.

The grieving process is ongoing and ever-changing. As caring adults, we need to create an understanding of the grieving child for parents, teachers, counselors, and other school personnel.

SYMPTOMS OF NORMAL GRIEF

BEHAVIOR

- sleeplessness
- loss of appetite
- poor grades
- crying
- nightmares
- dreams of deceased
- sighing
- listlessness
- absent mindedness
- clinging
- overactiveness
- social withdrawal
- verbal attacks
- fighting
- extreme quiet
- bed-wetting
- excessive touching
- excessive hugging

THOUGHT PATTERNS

- inability to concentrate
- difficulty making a decision
- self-destructive thoughts
- low self-image
- preoccupation
- confusion
- disbelief

FEELINGS

- anger
- guilt
- sadness
- mood swings
- depression
- hysteria
- relief
- helplessness
- fear
- loneliness
- anxiety
- rage
- intense feelings
- feeling unreal

PHYSICAL SYMPTOMS

- headaches
- fatigue
- shortness of breath
- dry mouth
- dizziness
- pounding heart
- hot or cold flashes
- heaviness of body
- sensitive skin
- increased illness
- empty feeling in body
- tightness in chest
- muscle weakness
- tightness in throat
- stomachaches

COMMON FEELINGS, THOUGHTS, AND BEHAVIORS OF THE GRIEVING CHILD

- Child retells *events* of the deceased's death and funeral.
- Child *dreams* of the deceased.
- Child *idolizes or imitates behaviors* of the deceased.
- Child *feels the deceased is with him or her* in some way.
- Child *speaks of his or her loved one in the present.*
- Child *rejects old friends and seeks new friends* who have experienced a similar loss.
- Child *wants to call home* during the school day.
- Child *can't concentrate* on homework or class work.
- Child *bursts into tears* in the middle of class.
- Child *seeks medical information* on death of deceased.

- Child *worries excessively* about his own health.
- Child sometimes *appears to be unfeeling* about loss.
- Child becomes the *"class clown"* to get attention.
- Child is *overly concerned* with caretaking needs.

COMMEMORATING

The third task of grief is commemoration. Children need to establish ways to remember the person or animal that died or the object that was lost or destroyed. *Involve* kids in formal and informal ways to commemorate. Their creative ideas are an essential part of this process.

FORMAL COMMEMORATION

Schools, camps, and community groups can arrange memorial services, commemorative plaques, or tributes in a yearbook.

Scholarship funds, donations to a particular charity, or a memorial garden can be established.

INFORMAL COMMEMORATION

Children can bring seeds to plant flowers honoring a principal, teacher, or student who died.

Children can choose a book to honor a child who was killed in an auto accident and donate the book to the library.

Children can create a school play and use the proceeds to begin a memorial fund in memory of a beloved teacher or classmate.

A class can decide what to do with the things inside the locker or desk of a student who has died. They can make a booklet of memories for his parents.

Sandra Fox, author of *Good Grief: Helping Groups of Children when a Friend Dies* (1988), emphasized that **"the life of every person who dies needs to be commemorated if we are to teach young people that all lives have value."** Many schools are afraid to acknowledge a suicide, thinking denial may prevent further occurrences. By remembering a "tragically too short life" rather than the way someone died, the school can create a teachable moment to talk to kids about how to recognize and work through feelings of pain and hopelessness.

GOING ON

The last psychological task for children experiencing significant loss is one that emphasizes going on with fun activities. Kids can begin to risk loving again and enjoying life. This does not mean forgetting the person who's gone or the object (i.e., a toy or a pet). Going on means developing a readiness to participate. Sometimes it signals a release of some of the deep guilt that is often felt.

Ann's dad had been dead for two years. She finally thought, "I don't need to visit dad's grave so much. I can remember him in my mind a lot." She now feels ready to go to the park where she spent so much time with Dad or let her Uncle Michael take her for ice cream the way Dad did.

Henry, whose best friend died in a car accident, tells his mom, "I want to go out with my friends again. We were talking about how much fun we had with Bill when he was alive, and we decided to go swimming where we used to go with him." The boys spent the day at the pool, reminiscing about old times with their friend.

 Understanding, grieving, commemorating, and going on are important parts of the child's process of loss, change, and growth. Recognizing these tasks can create a richer picture of where the child is in his or her process. Caring adults can see if a child is stuck in one particular task and help him or her to work with and through the grief.

The Story of Star

Star was Tom's pet dog. He was hit by a car and severely injured with no chance of recovery while Tom, a second grader, was at school. He came home and his dog was gone. He needed to understand why. His mom tells him, "Star was put to sleep." Tom imagines he will wake up soon and Star will be back. Mom says, "No, he's gone forever." Tom begins to worry that if he goes to sleep he, too, might not come back.

There's a better way to help Tom grieve.

It's OK for him to see his mom crying because she saw Star's favorite ball. She loved him too. Kids need explanations of what is happening so that the missing pieces won't be filled in with their own unrealistic imagination and interpretation.

Give young children the simplest information possible while still sharing needed facts for their growth. "How did Star die? What did the vet do? Who took him to the vet? Did he cry? Where was he buried? Can I see?" All of these questions need to be answered. Finally we need to say, "Star won't be back. We won't see him again. His body has stopped working. It is very sad and we will miss him very much. We can give Star a funeral and say goodbye to him."

Tom needs to work through the various feelings associated with grieving. He needs to

1. understand that the loss is real,

2. feel the hurt,

3. learn to live life without the loss object, and

4. transform the emotional energy of grief into life again.

LET KIDS KNOW

"Star won't be in your daily life, but he will be in your memory."

LET KIDS TALK

"I'm sad, angry, or frightened about what happened to Star. I feel so lonely without him."

LET KIDS PARTICIPATE

Tom can choose what to do with Star's toys, his bowl, or his collar. Where should we put his pictures? What kind of a ceremony would he like to have? Who would he like to invite?

LET KIDS BE UNIQUE

Each child is different and so is his or her grief. Tom wants to build a doghouse where Star is buried. It's Tom's own way of remembering Star.

Tom can commemorate Star's death informally or with a real ceremony. As long as Tom is involved, if he wants to be, he will be able to work through his grief. In his way, he can affirm the value of the life that was Star's. Tom decided to invite his family, neighborhood friends, and two pet dogs in the neighborhood. He read a poem, played music, and planted flowers as a tribute. He put a picture of Star by his bed to help remember him.

Once Tom has understood, grieved, and commemorated his dog's death, he will be ready to "go on." This readiness involves knowing it's OK to start life again—to play with other dogs or even hope to get a new one. Going on is not the same thing as forgetting. Star will live in Tom's heart. It may hurt on Star's birthday or the day that he died, yet Tom's grief experiences with Star will strenghten his ability to cope with other losses that he will assuredly have as life goes on.

CHAPTER 4

Techniques for Grief Work

IDENTIFY FEELINGS • LETTERS • DRAMA
PUPPETS • ART • MUSIC • CLAY • SAND TABLE
QUESTIONS • ROLE-PLAYING • JOURNALS
MEMORY BOOKS • MEMORY BOXES

Identify Feelings

Children under stress tend to cut themselves off from the "now," becoming often only half here. As caring adults, we can draw upon many techniques that will enable children to become more in touch with all aspects of themselves and to directly communicate with others by being fully and completely present.

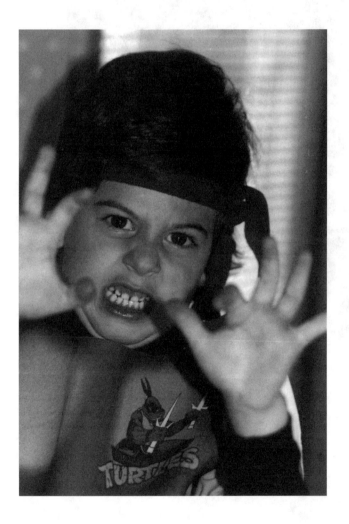

ANGER

"How could Daddy have died and left me all alone?"

Children often feel angry about the death or illness of a loved one. Losses such as divorce, moving, or the death of a pet or people certainly provoke anger. Feeling they have no control over what has happened, kids may project their angry feelings onto the person or thing that's gone, doctors, teachers, parents, siblings, or God.

Kids learn at a young age not to express anger. They push it inwards in order to get their needs met and to avoid being rejected or abandoned. Violet Oaklander, gestalt therapist and author of *Windows to Our Children* (1969), stressed that **"anger is an expression of self."**

If a child holds back and holds in his anger, he gives his personal power away by projecting his real feelings onto another person or object. Sammy had been fighting on the playground a lot. His teacher asked, "Why?" "All the kids are mean," Sammy replied. Sammy's underlying anger was a dad who had abandoned him. He kicked and hit the kids on the playground instead.

Adults can help kids by acknowledging their angry feelings and guiding them to say, "I'm angry." Let them know it's OK to feel anger and own it as theirs. "It's OK that I'm angry."

WE CAN BUILD AN ANGER AWARENESS BY TALKING WITH CHILDREN.

- What is anger?
- How does your body feel?
- What could make you angry?
- How do you show anger?
- What do you do when your angry?

Children can then use new skills to incorporate their anger. One productive expression of anger is direct communication—talking to the person with whom you are angry and telling him or her why you are angry. Another way to express anger personally is by taking the angry energy when it can't be expressed directly and using it in good ways.

Kids can take their anger and work with it in appropriate ways. They can vent angry energy by punching a pillow, building a project, using physical activity, role-playing, drawing, writing, or talking to a friend or adult.

I won't go to Grandma's. You could die while I'm away... like dad did!

PANIC

"Mommy, are you going to die too?"

Young children may have a huge fear of abandonment if one parent dies or leaves the house. They are afraid that if one parent has gone, the other could go, too. They may cling to the remaining parent, refusing to play with friends or do other activities. Children need to rebuild trust. It takes time.

DENIAL

"I can't believe Grandpa died. He couldn't have died. He'll be back."

Death, illness, or other loss can come as a surprise, and children as well as adults are shocked. If these experiences are overwhelming, kids may push them away as temporary relief from grief. Respect this as the child's way of saying what he or she can handle.

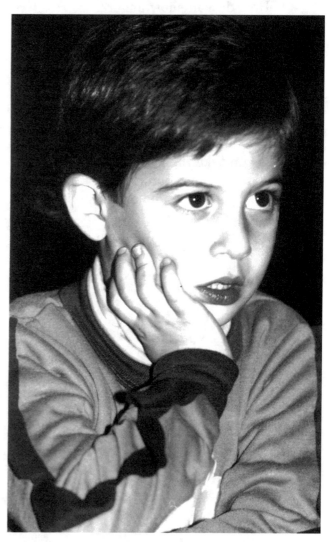

GUILT

Mom frowns. Ben thinks, *"I must have done something wrong to make her so angry. It's my fault. I've been such a bad kid lately!"*

He didn't understand Mom had just heard bad news on the telephone. Children can't separate themselves from the experience. They take in the adult messages, "swallow it," and "stuff it," sometimes carrying these messages all of their lives. Many of us live with the belief system of a four-year-old. We carry traumatic messages from early childhood, not only as if they were true then, but as if they are still true today.

WITHDRAWAL

"I won't go with the new gym teacher. I want to be alone."

Jason's mom's new boyfriend decided to stop being with Jason and his mom. Two years earlier Jason's dad had left town. Afraid to be vulnerable again, he withdrew from any new men that entered his life. The new gym teacher at school is a man. Jason refuses to go with the teacher and is sent to the principal's office for disobedience. No one understands that previous abandonment may have recreated Jason's fear of being hurt. Children may withdraw from loved ones as a safeguard against them leaving too. If kids have been traumatized too severely, they may be afraid to trust. Adults need to find creative ways to connect with children and build a relationship.

Stuffing the Feeling

Adults often urge children to stuff or deny their feelings because adults are uncomfortable with seeing those feelings in kids. *"What we resist, persists!"* The more we promote denial of feelings, the greater the feelings become.

Identifying the Feeling

When children's feelings are identified and given a name, those feelings are then validated. Although adults sometimes fear naming feelings will create a larger problem, it actually reduces the hurt by bringing it out into the open.

Grief Resolution Techniques: Ideas for All Ages

Techniques of grief resolution create and stimulate open discussion and exploration of feeling.

STORY TELLING

Begin a story with *"I wish"* or *"If only"* or *"Once upon a time there was a _____ who died* (got divorced, got sick, etc.). Each person in a small group continues the story.

Have children create this story: *Pretend you are an alien trying to find out what death is on earth* (Possible details—final, stop breathing, mystery, universal, happens to everyone, out of control).

CREATIVE WRITING

- letters to loved ones
- pictures and stuffed animals for projective story writing
- feeling journals
- diaries

- poetry
- essays
- memory books
- autobiographies

Letters to loved ones

Letters to loved ones are a useful tool to work through held-in thoughts and feelings. Using specific headings such as "Dear Mom" or "Dear Uncle Tom" helps kids really project themselves into the letter. Be sure they understand the loved one is not really getting the letter, and give the child a choice in the decision of what they want to do with it—put it somewhere special, share it, etc.

Dr. Lori Weiner, Coordinator of the Pediatric HIV Psychosocial Support Program, American Cancer Institute, generously donated the following letter and drawing. Her work with children and AIDS has led her to feel that "the most exquisite, intense, intimate, and painful life experiences have been those where we have been given the opportunity to give to another human being and the strength to let go and say goodbye" (*Social Work*, Sept. 1991, 375–388).

Sara's dad died of AIDS. Her mom is HIV infected and so is Sara. Sara has two siblings. She is ten years old.

Dear Mom,

I miss you. Sometimes I get scared when you get sick. I worry that you will not come home. I want you to take care of yourself. If you ever got real sick will you tell us? I worry too much. I worry about you because you might get sick, not tell me and die. If you died I would really be upset and sad and cry a whole lot. I cried last night because I missed you so much. Sometimes I worry about me getting sick too and what you would do if I got real sick. Like would you cry or would you come see me in the hospital? If you were in the hospital I want to come see you.

Sometimes I even think about heaven. It is quiet and peaceful there and I know that you and I will be there together one day.

Mommy I love you and know you love me.

Sara

ME and MOMMY in Heaven

Ashley's mom died, at age 29, of a sudden heart attack. Ashley was six years old.

Dear <u>Mom</u>,
I really miss you.
I am doing fine in school. I think about you everyday. I am really sorry you had to go down there. I wouldn't like it there myself. I don't know yet what to give you for mother's day.

Love,
Ashly

LETTER WRITING

Letter writing is a wonderful grief resolution technique for people from 3 years old to 103. It allows the expression of feelings and the ability to have an ongoing, everpresent internal relationship with a loved one that can continue to grow and develop.

A well-known celebrity explained in an interview his secret for keeping his son alive. When his son died, he was inundated with grief. He began to write him letters and mail them. In ten years he has written hundreds of letters, and continues to mail them. *"It's the only thing that helps to keep him alive for me."*

Joey's dad died of a sudden heart attack while he was playing baseball. Joey was playing at another game and wasn't there when his dad died. He explained, "If only I had been there, I could have saved his life." He missed his dad and wanted to write him a letter. He expressed his deep regret that he wished he could have saved him, and would spend all of his allowance if only that would bring him back.

Dear Dad,

I love you a lot! I wish you could come back and if I could see you and start all over again—I'd take you to the doctor and pay my life savings.

Love,

Joey

Eight-year-old Jackie's mom had died of a sudden heart attack and Jackie, her 15-year-old brother Alan, and dad were inundated with grief. After one year, the family began to feel like they could begin to live life in a different way. Dad began dating a woman named Ann. Several weeks later Jackie burst into our grief therapy session filled with tears, with dad in the waiting room.

"What is so upsetting?" I asked. "I don't want my father dating Ann. I hate it! I hate it!" she screamed. "Why don't you write your dad a letter about how you feel? You don't have to show it to him but you can if you want to."

She began writing the following letter. Many children have these feelings when a surviving parent begins dating.

> Dear Dad,
> I don't want to share you. I'm afraid that I will lose you too.
> Love, Jackie

She chose to share the letter with her dad. This concrete tool proved effective in creating a dialogue about her mom's death and her dad's dating.

Tara was a nine-year-old who had recently experienced the death of her grandmother and missed her very much. She worried excessively about the health of her parents, a very common sign of the grieving child. One day she came to a therapy session, very concerned and upset with her dad for not wearing his seat belt. I suggested she write a letter to her dad telling him how she feels, and she even put a reply box on the letter for her dad to answer.

Dear Dad,
    Please start
Wearing your seat
belt all the time.
I want you to wear
your seat belt all
the time because
it's safe. If you don't
When you get in an
accident you might
get hurt. I worry
about that.

a. yes
b. no
c. maybe
d. sometimes
e. will try

Circle One

Please write back
and return in
pocket on back.

Love,
Tara

Wear your
    Belt!

DAD

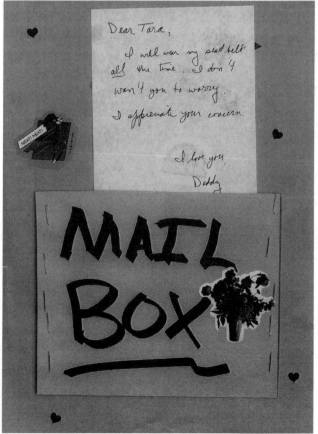

Dear Tara,
    I will wear my seat belt
all the time. I don't
want you to worry.
I appreciate your concern.

    I love you,
        Daddy

MAIL
BOX

Eleven-year-old Roxanne was grieving the recent deaths of three of her grandparents. She also worried excessively about her dad's health, especially his smoking. The following is a letter she wrote to Dad explaining her feelings and concerns about his health.

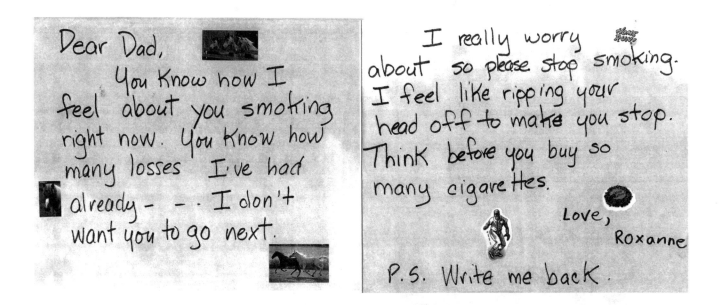

Dear Dad,
You know how I feel about you smoking right now. You know how many losses I've had already - - - I don't want you to go next.

I really worry about so please stop smoking. I feel like ripping your head off to make you stop. Think before you buy so many cigarettes.

Love,
Roxanne

P.S. Write me back.

Poetry

Kim is a 16-year-old who loves her grandfather very much. After living with his long and serious illness, she remained by his bed during his final hours. This poem is her way of expressing her deep and powerful emotions as she experienced being with him at the time of his death.

All I Could Say

by Kimberly Seff

I love you was all I could say.
He did not cry, He felt my pain.
On his bed where he lay,
I held his hand as he slipped away.
I love you was all I could say.
Have a great life.
Don't change a thing.
You're perfect in my eyes, deeply from within.
Are you alright?
Please tell me the truth.
Take care of Red for me.
She needs your love and frolicsome youth.
I want to go home now where I can be free.
From this wretched moroseness and fervent agony.

Don't miss me too much,
I will never really leave.
My soul and spirit will live on in your memory.
Looking down at him with a congenial smile,
Attempting to hide my tears and my sadness.
It was emphatic as to what the future foretold . . and still
I love you was all I could say.
His spirit flutters around me like an elegant butterfly.
Soaring like a sparrow through the winter sky.
Overlooking and protecting the life and love he left behind.
The missing and all the memories are running through my mind.
The tears flow like rivers in the darkness where no one can see.
How I sulk in my own misery.
A saint in my eyes due to gallantry ways, but
I told him "I love you" and "Ditto" was all he could say.
—In loving memory of Bill Seff

Essays

Essays can be used as grief resolution techniques. Not only do these essays allow students to express their feelings, but teachers and college personnel can know and understand how profoundly these loss and grief experiences affect the lives of these kids and assuredly shape who they are.

Eric Dreisen, a 15-year-old, wrote the following article in his school newspaper after his mom's death. He hoped to reach out to other teens who had also experienced the death of someone close to them.

Help With Tough Times

by Eric Dreisen '95

As some of you might be aware, my mother passed away from cancer this school year. In experiencing this loss, there have been some positive things that have come from it. I have learned to take care of myself, my family and friends have become more important, and I have learned to help other people who are going through tough times.

The purpose of this article is to invite any student who is suffering from a loss or who is going through tough times, to meet on a regular basis as a group to talk about the problem. I will organize this group by having speakers come or get information to help with this long, hard process. Please contact me at ____ _____ .

The following essay was written by Allison Rothenberg, a 17-year-old junior in high school. She was asked to write, as a college entrance requirement, about an important experience that greatly affected her life. She wrote the following warm and sensitive tribute to her dad, Alan, who died when she was seven.

Ten years ago, my father, Alan Lee Rothenberg, died. He was my best friend when I was seven years old. He became sick and had to go into the hospital. I asked my mom, "Is he going to die?" She said, "Of course not," and told me not to think like that again.

His death shocked me, and no one in my family expected something so tragic to happen. After all my dad died at the early age of thirty-nine. When my mother told my brother and me, we were stunned. My brother, Andy, was only four and didn't understand but knew something bad had happened. I thought it was a nightmare, I couldn't comprehend it. The thought of his death scared me. I didn't even know what to say, but when I realized it was true I cried my eyes out. I remember my mom and I cried so much that we went through a whole box of kleenex.

I kept my feelings inside me for a long time, but as I got older and began to understand "why" it became easier to express how I felt. I'm so grateful that we spent special moments together. Things like driving his car while I was sitting on his lap in an empty parking lot or trying on his shoes and acting like a clown. We'd always end up laughing and spending unforgettable times together.

I remember my dad told me to strive for the best, and if I really out my mind to it, my wished would come true. Well, two birthdays had gone by and the only thing that I wished for on my candles was to have my dad come back. This was one of the only wishes that never came true and the most important.

I miss him a lot, but I know he's out there somewhere looking out for me and guiding me in the right direction. I still feel there is a part of him with me—after all, we both have the same middle name, and my family and friends always tell me and my brother how much we resemble my dad.

Thanks to my dad's saying, "Strive for the best," I never settle for anything but that. His words keep me moving. Even though he's gone, I always have the memories. Those will never die.

Pictures for Projective Techniques

Pictures and storytelling can be used as a projective technique. They allow children to safely express feelings. Consider the following examples.

Jerry's brother Greg was killed in a plane crash. He put his brother's favorite hat on his dog, Casper, and then began to say . . .

Mr. Squirrel was sitting on the post thinking about Mr. Rabbit, his best friend, who went away for the Fall. All of a sudden he got the idea to write him a letter. What do you think he is going to say?

Tom and Jim went up to the tree house after their dog, Rex, was hit by a car and killed. What do you think they are talking about?

GENEOGRAMS

Seth's sister Donna died of leukemia when Seth was seven. Donna was eighteen. Now Seth is ten and exploring Donna's death as well as other losses in his family. The geneogram, a pictorial family history, helped him to see which family members have died, which ones are still living, and which family members are those he can and cannot depend on. When Seth circled his Grandma Rose as someone he couldn't depend on, I questioned him about it. "What is it you can't depend on?" I asked. "Her memory," he replied. "She has Alzheimer's."

This geneogram helped to create a teachable moment with the use of a wonderful resource, "Always Grandma" a book for children about a grandmother with Alzheimer's. Seth loved the book and asked if he could borrow it to share with his mom. His mother called a few days later to say the book was a true gift. It explained in simple words many of the losses she was feeling constantly living with her mom's disease, and asked if she could share this resource with her adult siblings. **Sometimes children's literature provides a useful tool for all members of the family to begin a dialogue about their common loss issues.**

Children's Questions and Techniques for Answering Them

I. QUESTIONS FOR GOD

WHY DID YOU HAVE TO KILL MY MOTHER?

Four years after Ryan's dad died in an airplane crash, he asked this question for the first time. "You must be pretty angry at God," I commented. "I am!" he declared. Then we began to talk about his anger. I handed Ryan some clay and he began to form figures of God and an airplane. "Why did you do this?" he cried, and the tears began to release his anger. He smashed both figures, screaming "I hate you, why did you kill my mother?" Then he slumped, whispering, "It's not God's fault, it's nobody's fault." This was the beginning of the meltdown process.

2. QUESTIONS FOR A MOM THAT DIED

WHAT DID IT FEEL LIKE TO DIE? (AND DID YOU THINK ABOUT ME?)

Gina feels lonely after her mom died and wonders if Mom thought about her when she died. We can talk about her feelings of abandonment and rejection caused by death, and her worry that Mom may have suffered. "What do you imagine?" I asked. "I imagine she was bleeding and in a lot of pain," she responded. "Let's write down some questions and ask dad to write the answers. Then you will know." Sometimes children imagine far worse than if they know the truth. Some of Gina's questions were:

- What did mom look like?
- Did the doctor say Mom was in pain?
- What did the doctor say?
- Did you see her die?

3. QUESTIONS ABOUT FORGETTING

WILL I FORGET MY MOM?

Ted is afraid he will forget his Mom. He tries to remember her voice, but sometimes gets scared he can't hear it in his mind. At night before he goes to bed, he wants to picture her face. Sometimes he can't. I can invite Ted to replay the homevideo of mom, bring in a photo album about her, or draw a picture of her. He can also ask friends and relatives to send him a picture of her that he has never seen and tell him a new memory.

4. QUESTIONS ABOUT CLICHÉS

WHY DO PEOPLE ALWAYS SAY ONLY THE GOOD DIE YOUNG?

"Even though my mom was 30 when she died, my grandmother is good and now she's 78. I'm only eight. Does that mean that God will take me? That makes me scared." Sally then began to explain her terror that she might die young like her mom. Only then could we begin to examine this magical thinking by exploring the facts about her mom's death.

5. QUESTIONS ABOUT CLOSURE

CAN I VISIT THE PLACE WHERE MY BROTHER WAS KILLED?

Mary's brother, Adam, was murdered randomly by a neighborhood gang while walking home from work late one night. Mary needed to go back to the scene of the crime and see where the murder took place. She asked her boyfriend to bring her there, retracing every step of the murder account that she had read in a newspaper until she felt she had relived it. "Suddenly I felt Adam was with me, and I was glad I was there."

6. QUESTIONS ABOUT SECRECY

"WHY DOESN'T ANYONE TALK ABOUT DAD?"

Peggy's dad died when she was ten years old and no one in her family ever talks about him. She, her brother, and mom never say a word about his death. He had committed suicide. Now Peggy is 15. "I miss my dad so much, but even more I miss being able to talk about him. I feel so alone." I suggested she might like to join a support group for suicide survivors as a way to feel less alone and to be with people that can understand her experience.

7. QUESTIONS ABOUT FACTS

WHAT EXACTLY HAPPENED WHEN MY DAD DIED?

JoAnne heard lots of different stories about her dad's fatal car crash when she was six years old. At age 13, she asked the question above for the first time. She explained she wanted to know the facts and asked if she could look up the account of the accident in the newspaper so that she could really know what happened. We examined the newspaper article together and recorded a list of facts and misconceptions and discussed the similarities and differences. Now, at a different developmental stage, she was ready to regrieve the death in a new and age-appropriate way—discovering concrete facts about her dad's death.

8. QUESTIONS ABOUT THE INABILITY TO GRIEVE OPENLY

WHY DON'T I CRY ANYMORE?

Donna explained that she used to cry and complain a lot before her Dad died. She was nine. Now she is 15 and she says she never cries. "I wonder why?" she asked me one day. I asked Donna if anyone had ever given her the message that crying wasn't good. She relayed a powerful story. After the funeral her sister, Beverly, told her "You need to be strong and take care of Mom now because you are the only one home with her." "I guess strong meant not to cry. I never realized that before." Donna told me in astonishment. This was her first step towards releasing her hidden tears. She begin to bring in pictures of her life with her dad. In this safe environment, we explored her repressed sadness of Dad's death and how much she misses him.

9. QUESTIONS ABOUT DYING

WILL YOU DIE TOO?

Sara worried excessively about her parents health after the death of her grandmothers. She feared her mom and dad would die too. We made a "worry box" with magazine pictures showing her worries. Sara wrote them and put them in the box. Both of her parents also got medical checkups, and each doctor wrote a note to Sara confirming their good health. Here's one of them.

 Dear Sara,
I am pleased to report to you that after doing a complete medical exam, with lots of tests and examinations, your dad is very healthy and seems to be in great shape. If you have any questions, please let me know.
Love,
Dr. Brenner

10. QUESTIONS ABOUT MAGICAL THINKING

IS IT MY FAULT MY DAD DIED?

Henry's dad took him to the park when he was four. He and Dad sat down on the park bench. Henry's dad shot himself in the head in front of Henry. Henry's mom continually told him it was his fault, because he did not stop his dad. As a teenager Henry was obsessed with wanting to murder someone, so "he could know what it feels like."

II. QUESTIONS ABOUT HEAVEN

WHAT IS HEAVEN?

Michelle wondered what heaven was like. She decided to write a story about it and draw the following picture to explain what she feels heaven is like. It helped her express a lot of ideas about where her mom was, and how she felt heaven was a safe and wonderful place. She also got to share more about her mom with me that I didn't know.

What Is Heaven?

This is what heaven is to me. It's a beautiful place. Everyone is waiting for a new person, so they can be friends. They are also waiting for their family. They are still having fun. They get to meet all the people they always wanted to meet (like Elvis). There are lots of castles where only the great live, like my Mom. There's all the food you want and all the stuff to do — There's also dancing places, disco. My mom loved to dance. I think she's dancing in heaven.

Animals are always welcome. (My Mom loved animals.) Ask her how Trixie is. That's her dog that died.

Tell her I love her

Michelle Age 11

12. QUESTIONS ABOUT SAFETY

WHAT CAN YOU DO SO THAT I WILL FEEL YOU ARE SAFE?

Susie came to a grief therapy session very angry. "I won't let my dad go away with Tammy (his new girlfriend) for the weekend." She slammed the door and began to cry. "Why not?" I questioned. "I'm afraid he'll die too, just the way my mom did." Susie's mom had been killed in a sudden car crash. She was not wearing her seatbelt. "What could dad do in order for you to feel safe?" I asked. We brainstormed about it, and Susie came up with several ideas. She was afraid to tell Dad how she felt so she decided to write a letter.

> Dear Dad
> I am afraid you will get killed like mom did if you take the car away for the weekend. Please borrow Uncle Tom's Jeep. It's new and it has airbags. Don't speed, and wear your seatbelt.
> Love,
> Susie
> PS. Will you call me when you get there?

I asked Susie permission to share the letter with her dad and she gave it. Dad first thought it didn't make sense, but soon realized her fears stemmed from Mom's death. He agreed to borrow Uncle Tom's van, wear his seat belt, and call at a designated time. Susie felt more in control now that her feelings were validated and she had a plan.

MEMORY WORK

Memory Boxes

Memory boxes are an excellent craft project for grieving children. Children can collect special articles that belonged to or remind them of the person that died. These objects can be put in a shoe box and decorated by the child as a valuable treasure of memories. It also can serve as a tool for stimulating conversation.

Jonathan's favorite uncle, George, died of cancer when he was nine. He decided to make a memory box and decorate it with stickers and pictures that reminded him of his uncle. He then placed a very precious object inside, Uncle George's karate certificate for being a black belt. It served as an inspiration as well as ongoing place to be with his uncle's memory.

Picture Albums

Often I have found that creating "My Life" picture albums with children is an extremely useful tool in creating dialogue and sharing feelings. Mary's dad died of cancer when she was 10. I invited her to choose pictures she loved and make an album about her life before and after her dad died. She chose each picture and we wrote a sentence about it.

Memory boxes and picture albums are important tools that enable children to share feelings and ideas. A memory table also allows kids to share meaningful objects that link them to loved ones.

Memory Mural or Collage

Children love to express memories through artwork. They can draw a memory mural or create a collage from magazine pictures that remind them of the person or pet that died. Eight-year-old Carol experienced the death of her cat, Samantha, when she was hit by a car and killed. Carol felt a tremendous loss in her life, and grieved her sweet pet for many months to come.

Carol made a memory collage using magazine pictures. She shared a lot about Samantha and how much she missed her.

Memory Pillow and Photographs

Murray was a beloved dog and friend to 12-year-old Ross and his 16-year-old sister, JoJo. Murray's dying process was slow and hard. The family surrounded him with love and cared for his needs until he died. Murray spent much of his last time on earth on his dog bed. Ross took the following picture of this and made copies to share with family and friends.

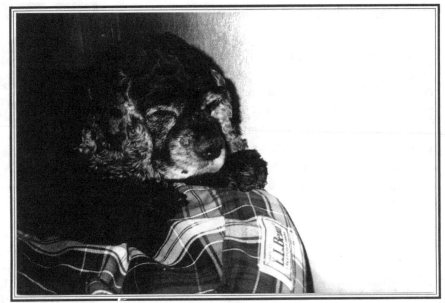

OLD DOG

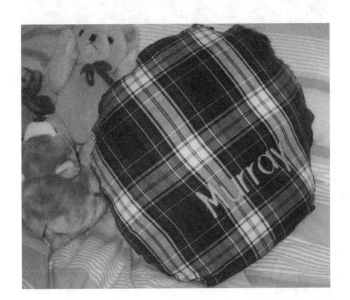

After Murray's death, JoJo's mom made a pillow from Murray's bed and out his name on it. She gave it to JoJo to take with her to college so that she would feel Murray was always with her.

Memory books

Memory books are extremely useful tools to allow children to express feelings and complete unfinished business (what they didn't get a chance to say). Children can express themselves through writing and drawing in age-appropriate ways. Inside the memory book, kids can use stars, stickers, photographs, and other decorations. There are many different kinds of pages kids can make. Here are a few suggestions.

- The most important thing I learned from the person is...

- Write a letter (Dear _____, Love _____)

- What is the funniest memory you have?

- My most special memory is...

- If you could tell your loved one just one more thing, what would you say? What do you think they would tell you?

- If there is one thing you are sorry for it would be...

The following are five memory book pages. They were donated by Allyson Nuggent, bereavement counselor at the Stella Marris Hospice in Baltimore, MD. The first picture was made by a 13-year-old boy after his father died of a heart attack. The boy illustrated his view of the funeral in great detail. The next picture shows a young girl's perception of life before and after her dad's suicide. The picture shows the troubled relationship with her mother since her father's death. A six-year-old girl explored her feelings about her dad's death in the following two pictures. The last picture shows how a 13-year-old remembers good things while grieving about her dad.

Family and Friends come to a funeral service to remember a special person and to show their love for you.

What did you see at the funeral?

The thing that worries me the most since the death of my person is . . .
becaues my family is sad.

This is a picture of what I am worried about

I Get Angry About
<u>they DiD not do anything</u> to him
since the death of my Person

I show my Anger by
<u>telling Someone</u>

This is me when I Am
! Angry !

Melissa is a 13-year-old whose father died of lung cancer. Her love for him shines through her warm memory of her dad.

My funniest memory of "my father is when . . ."

He came home from getting his hair shaved off after being diagnosed with lung cancer. During his cancer he always kept a good attitude. That's just my Dad's personallity.— a good sense of humor. Why do the good people have to die?

By Melissa Bradshaw
age 13

Ongoing Memory Work

Zacky's friend, Andrew, died when he was six. Now Zacky is nine. The following is a picture he drew for the cover of Andrew's third memorial booklet, "On the Occasion of Andrew's Third Anniversary." This drawing allowed Zacky to continue to actively remember his friend and participate in ongoing memory work.

"Andrew Shooting Baskets In Heaven"
Artist: Zachy Beauchamp Age 8

Memory e-mails are a creative example of memory work and computer use.

After Chelsea's classmate Ronald got killed in a car crash, she and her classmates decided to create e-mail memories. Each child began writing and sharing e-mails with the rest of the class about time spent and experiences with Ronald.

DRAMA AND IMAGINATION

Children use drama and imagination with props, costumes, and puppets to help them act out and identify feelings and thoughts. The young child can use the toy telephone to call someone who is gone. Kids can safely talk into a tape recorder to express unresolved feelings. Puppets are a wonderful tool to create an imaginary dialogue between a child and someone who has left. Dress up for young children is another technique enabling them to immerse themselves in role-playing, becoming the loved one or another member of the family. Children also can role-play with toy figures or figures in a sand table to show how they feel.

 Fantasy is a powerful tool for projection.

Stimulating Open Discussion

Photographs are a safe and natural way to communicate about the person who died. We can sometimes ask the children to help make scrapbooks about their loved one. This not only stimulates conversation but creates a memory to keep for years to come. Personal items specially chosen by the child that belonged to the deceased also are a wonderful remembrance and a way to keep getting to know what that person was like as the child gets older.

Locked diaries are a tool to create a space to write thoughts and feelings privately, with the availability to be shared at another time.

Punching bags and wrestling stuffed animals allow children to express anger and frustration in a safe way.

Polaroid pictures are good encouragement for open dialogue. By taking a polaroid picture of the child and placing it within one of his or her drawings, the child can project himself or herself into the drawing and begin to role-play.

Stuffed animals, puppets and grief dolls are a child-oriented projective technique to allow discussion and expression of feeling.

Putting thoughts and feelings into a tape recorder allows children to safely store or erase anything. It also gives them the choice to share if and when they are ready.

ART

The media of **art** also can promote open discussion and enhance open feelings. Children can:

- Draw the loss (death, divorce, moving, etc.).
- Draw how they would like it to be.
- Draw their house and who's inside.
- Draw "What Makes Me Batty." Kids write feeling words as they talk about what bothers them.
- Draw a mural of the common loss.
- Make a class booklet with words, pictures, poems, and photos.
- Draw scribbles on a large piece of paper. Let the child choose a section, create a drawing, and talk about it. Give the drawing a title. If it could talk, what would it say? The scribble becomes a story for discussion.

Children can choose from art materials, such as size and color of paper, and what kind of crayons, pens, or markers they want to use. As children draw we can ask:

"Do you mind if I watch you draw?"
"Can you tell me about your picture?"

Begin a dialogue that will create a story. The parent, teacher, or counselor can come closer to the picture to see if there is something in it the child can identify with and ask, "Tell me more about it." The child may realize then that the dog he or she drew in the picture is connected to him or her: "I'm like that dog. I bark at my sister all day."

 Interpretation has limited value to children. Even if it's correct, it may not help the child express his or her feelings. In griefwork, the most important aspect of artwork is freedom of expression without judgment.

Five-year-old Caroline was asked to answer the question "What is death?" She simply responded that death was her Grandma in a coffin. She drew the following picture that illustrates how she views death—Grandma lying inside of her coffin.

Grandma in her coffin

By Caroline   9/5/94

Caroline also remembers Grandma in happy ways. "Grandma gave me a happy book before she died. My happy book has pictures of Grandma and me."

CLAY

Clay is a very versatile medium to use with children. It is reusable and easy to work with. Kids can mold their family, friends, or animals, and create dialogues between themselves and others. Clay has a very calming effect for children, and they can gain a feeling of mastery by working with it. Kids interact with clay by pounding, squeezing, pinching, ripping, smoothing and poking it. Many feelings can be expressed in a safe way.

Joey made a figure of his deceased brother out of clay. When asked, "What would you like to say to him?" Joey began to say goodbye. "You were a good brother, sorry you had to die." Then he kissed the figure. Joey also made the doctors that took care of his brother. "I hate you!" he shouted, "You wouldn't let me scream." He began pounding the clay and smashing it to bits. He was using his clay as a good projective tool to express anger.

Five-year-old Kyle's baby brother died and Kyle's mom encouraged him to use clay to work with his feelings. He created a clay angel and gave his mom the following note:

This is My brother Andrew. He died after He was born. He was a twin.

MUSIC

Music can be used as a resource to explore feelings. Kids can listen to sounds that different instruments make to create feelings.

drums–anger   bells–sadness

harmonica–loneliness   harp–angel-like

cymbals–shock   tuba –awkwardness

Feelings can be projected into the music through body movement and dance. Doing so is very freeing to children. Hap Palmer's album, *"Feelings,"* is wonderful to use with young children.

For teens, Eric Clapton's *Tears In Heaven* and Elton John's *Goodbye English Rose* can provide music to relate to. These songs help evoke feelings that can create discussion and sharing.

IDENTIFYING FEELINGS

KIDS CAN IDENTIFY FEELINGS BY:

1. Painting a picture of the feeling. "How does your anger look when you mom yells at you?"
2. Keeping an ongoing notebook of feelings with writing and drawing.
3. Doing feeling homework. Make a list of what makes you angry, sad, afraid, frustrated, etc.
4. Creating the feeling our of sand, clay, or puppets.

PARENTS CAN HELP KIDS IDENTIFY FEELINGS BY:

1. Allowing kids to identify and express dislikes openly. Make up a game with them where they say what they don't like.
2. Having a "Mad Session." During the routine bedtime ritual, parents can ask "Is there anything that made you mad today?" Be sure not to make any judgments or comments on answers.
3. Practicing yelling "no!" or pounding on a pillow.
4. Reading books that open feelings discussion.
5. Talking about things. "What was your nightmare about last night? Let's see if you can draw what frightened you."

 An important part of all of these techniques is that they have projective value. Children can't easily integrate their emotions and their intellect. Our job as caring adults is to help children reach all the parts of themselves that may have been cut off. We can do this by creating a relationship where two people can interact in an atmosphere that honors and respects who they are.

Creating a Resource Library

A resource shelf at home or in school is very important for kids. Be sure to include age-appropriate children's literature on the grief and loss issue they are experiencing. Here are some suggestions:

Be a Bird, Be a Frog, Be a Tree by Rachel Carr (1973). A picture guide for using creative movement (yoga) with young children.

Put Your Mother on the Ceiling by Richard De Milleis (1973). Another good resource filled with children's imagination games.

The Creative Journal for Children by Lucia Capacchione (1982). A guide using writing and drawing to promote kid's self-esteem.

The Hurt by Teddi Doleski (1983). The wonderful story of a boy who keeps all of his hurts inside, until the hurt grows so big it fills his room. When he shares his feelings, the hurt begins to go away.

When Dinosaurs Die (1996) by Laura and Marc Brown. This is a practical guide for children to understand death.

MEMORY BOOK RESOURCES

Bart Speaks Out on Suicide by Linda Goldman (1998) is a memory book that children can interact with that speaks to the topic of suicide.

Changing Faces by Donna O'Toole (1995) is an interactive memory book for pre-teens and teens that gives clear explanations about grief.

Fire In My Heart, Ice in My Veins by Enid Traisman (1992) is a memory book that allows children to actively participate in the grieving process.

When Someone Very Special Dies, When Mom and Dad Separate, and *When Someone Has a Very Serious Illness* are a series of excellent interactive memory books by Marge Heegaard (1988).

C H A P T E R   5

Preparing for a Goodbye Visit

YOU KNOW
   GRANDPA IS
   VERY SICK
HE'S GOING TO DIE
   SOON
HE PROBABLY
   WON'T TALK
   MUCH
HE LOOKS TERRIBLE

Let's Prepare Kids to Say Goodbye

Preparing a child for a goodbye visit to a dying loved one is a topic that is usually avoided or denied in our culture. A visit to an aging, sickly grandparent can be approached in a sensitive way.

To include children in the decision making is important. Does the child want to visit the ill person? If he or she answers "no," find out what the fears are. If discussed openly, these fears could be eliminated. If the child decides to go, talk about the hospital and the room where the sick person will be. Explain how he or she will look and his or her physical appearance may have changed with the illness. Suggest bringing a gift to the loved one. It's another way of saying goodbye. Make visits brief and provide space, both in time and location, for kids to discuss, write, or draw how they feel after their visit.

To prepare kids for the visit we need to be honest in language and feelings. Kids can, and often do, model themselves after the adults.

"Grandpa had a heart attack last night. He is very sick." Mom explains. Ben asked a very common and direct question, "Will Grandpa die?" "He may," his mom answered, adding hopefully, "but the doctors are working very hard to make him well again! I was scared when I heard about Grandpa, and very sad," Mom confided. "Is that how you feel? What can I do to help you?"

Because adults are often not sure what to say, it is necessary to have comfortable language to use.

PREPARING CHILDREN FOR A GOODBYE: ONE FAMILY'S STORY

The following is a wonderful account of how a family approached their goodbye visit. "Preparing a Child for a Goodbye Visit" is an article written by Judith Rubenstein, *JAMA*, May 14, 1982 Vol. 247, pp. 2571–2572 (Copyright 1982, American Medical Association). It illustrates a farewell to a grandfather dying of cancer. The children, ages four and six, were prepared by the parents. Their mother tells the story.

The Situation

There was no denying Grandpa was dying. My husband, who rarely travels, was suddenly making frequent short trips to Chicago to visit him. The children overheard the anxious, daily, long-distance telephone calls to or from my mother-in-law, and afterwards the anxious conversations between my husband and me.

The children had a loving relationship with their Grandpa, built on pleasant visits several times a year when Grandma and Grandpa would come to Boston from Chicago. I remember in particular tireless sessions teaching toddlers to walk, and then later, long intimate walks, sometimes including "rest stops" at the candy or toy store.

Because of this warm relationship, we felt that the older children were entitled to say good-bye to him.... We decided I would take our 6-year-old daughter to Chicago on one trip, and my husband would take our 4-year-old son on a separate trip.

Many people, friends, and family, strongly objected. They said, "Let them remember him the way he was." "He has deteriorated, and his changed appearance will frighten them." We rejected this well-meaning counsel in the belief that children have to learn that, however sad, sickness ending in death is part of life and that human beings have a need to say good-bye when time shared is over, whether it is a short, social visit or life itself.

Our Words

My husband and I together spoke to each child alone. We chose the time after breakfast one morning, since our children were most refreshed and alert at that time of day. Also, they has the rest of the day to think and ask questions. (Speaking of such an emotional concept in the evening would only have upset bedtime.) Our presentation to each child took only five or ten minutes, including questions from the child and repetitions by us. We began something like this:

> *"We have something important to talk to you about. Come and sit on my lap. I'm going to Chicago in a few days to see Grandpa, and I'd like to take you with me, if you want to go. Before you decide, listen to what we have to say."*

The children wanted to go. They responded to our statements as we made them, and my husband and I backtracked and repeated, and our presentation was not a smooth monologue, but we did speak the following phrases in more or less the following order:

> *You know Grandpa is very sick. He's going to die soon.*
>
> *This is probably the last time you are going to see him.*
>
> *He's changed a lot since you saw him last.*
>
> *He looks terrible.*
>
> *He's very thin. He's very pale. He's very weak.*
>
> *He probably won't talk much. He may cry.*
>
> *But you don't have to be afraid.*
>
> *He's still your same Grandpa.*
>
> *He's unhappy because he knows he's going to be dying soon, and he doesn't want to leave us.*
>
> *You may give him a big hug and kiss.*
>
> *It will make him feel better.*
>
> *You don't have to be afraid to kiss him.*
>
> *You can't catch his sickness. It's not a kind of sickness you can catch.*
>
> *You love your Grandpa and he loves you.*
>
> *You may tell him you love him if you want to.*
>
> *That will make him feel good, too.*

Following our explanation, each child asked more questions. Both children wanted to be reassured that they wouldn't catch any "germs" from Grandpa, and we repeated that his illness didn't have germs one could catch. Then the conversation turned to details of travel in the airplane, who else we would see in Chicago, and more questions about "germs." Then, before the questions and repetitions became too great, and the emotional tension turned to annoyance, we ended the conversation with:

> We have talked enough for now. If you have any more questions or if you want to talk about it again, you can ask us later. You can go play now.

Throughout the day and the following ones, the children asked questions from time to time, while I was preparing a meal or folding laundry, or doing some quiet task not focused on the child, and we discussed the idea again, but in a more casual way.

The Visit

A few days later, when my 6-year-old daughter and I visited my father-in-law, he was in pajamas in a wheelchair in the hospital waiting room. A compassionate physician and a humane hospital policy made this possible. My daughter approached him with poised self-confidence and affection, without fear, lugubriousness, or false cheerfulness. She said, "Hi, Grandpa." She reached up and put her arms around his neck and kissed his cheek. She smiled coyly and handed him a slip of paper on which she had drawn a picture and written, "I love you."

Grandpa and granddaughter hugged each other and smiled. The old man started to cry, and the little girl slipped down and sat on a chair. The adults talked a little while longer, and then we left. As I pushed open the heavy glass doors to leave, my daughter turned and waved good-bye to Grandpa and followed me, skipping and smiling. The next week, my husband told me that he and our 4-year-old son had a similar experience at their visit.

In the years following my father-in-law's death, our children have mentioned that last visit from time to time. Although their remembrance of specific details, including their conversation, has blurred, they speak of the visit with a certain wistful pleasure which makes us happy that we did not deny it to them.

Source: *JAMA.* May 14, 1982, Vol. 247. No. 18. Reprinted with permission.

GOODBYE VISIT MEMORIES

 Lindsey had visited with her Grandpa as he was dying when she was seven-years-old. At age nine, she has expressed her memories of her goodbye visit with her grandfather and her experience of his death through the poem *Grandpa*.

Grandpa

by: Lindsey Reynolds, Age 9

There he lays sick
He was sick for a long time.
But this time the sickest
My mom's sisters, cousins, aunts, uncles
Everyone was there, quiet hoping
praying his heartbeat will quicken
Silence no one talks, just watching
my Grandpa laying on his white
silky sheets wanting to reassure
everyone he was going to be okay
but he couldn't cancer the horrible
demon wouldn't let him get off
that easy. He should've been in the
hospital everybody said no he has to
be in his own bed, his own house when
angels blow their holy trumpets and
sweep him off to heaven suddenly
Aunt Judy talks she says "This is a time
for dad, he needs us" that might have
not been what she said but I
sort of felt her saying it in my
heart. At the time I was
at home with my dad and sister watching
TV. But back at Grandpa's house no
  happiness
through the room just love and worriedness
It was strange Grandpa knew everyone
knew he was going to die tonight but
everyone knew he wasn't worried or
was he. We could see a twinkle in his

eyes his eyes weren't open but you could feel it
was his last moments
alive he wanted to
spend it all with his daughters.
Suddenly his heart stopped
his heart was so tired to old to stay alive
it needed its eternal sleep and
so did Grandpa. Suddenly his silky
white sheets turned into angels that
put him on their back and carried
him off. Then one of the people said
that he was gone. Everyone cried a little.
After the crying the phone call to my
Dad when my dad picked up he talked
then he said his apologies then I knew
I took the phone and said Grandpa died
didn't he when mom said yes
I wanted to cry but I knew
I had to be strong.

Saying Goodbye at the Funeral Home

The funeral home can be a place that kids are allowed to say goodbye in a very child oriented way. An innovative funeral home asked me to help them create a children's room, where boys and girls could play, write goodbye letters to loved ones, and make goodbye items out of clay to place in the casket. The funeral director spoke of the enormous appreciation of parents for having a safe haven within the funeral home. Children could stay in this special room with supervision if they chose to leave the service.

The children's room was equipped with materials for children to express feelings, whether through play, writing, or drawing. Many puppets were available, as well as blocks and trucks. Books on death and loss issues were placed throughout the room for kids at different developmental stages, as well as resources for parents. Children expressed their grief in different ways. Tom wrote a letter to Mom and placed it in the casket. Susan made a heart out of clay. Alex used the dog puppet to talk about her sadness. Jerry and Alice watched a video about a cat named Barney that died.

Saying Goodbye at the Memorial Service

Sometimes children can't have the opportunity of saying goodbye. The loved one dies unexpectedly. Bobby died suddenly, leaving his four children no opportunity for a goodbye visit. They actively participated in saying goodbye at the memorial service by writing the following note to their dad that was a special part of the funeral service booklet that day.

Good Daddy

*We thought you would
be with us for years to
come,
But we know that you
are happy wherever you
are.
We love you from all of
our hearts.*

Pat, Jackie, Bobby, and Tiffany

Do Talk with Children About Death

WAYS THAT WORK

Realize grief is an ongoing process with no easy answers.

Allow new loss to be the first priority with a child's classmates.

Trust your instincts.

Initiate discussions of loss issues if the child does not.

Encourage children to attend the funeral, if they choose.

Consider ways to commemorate loss (bulletin board displays, letters to family, letters to person who died, photographs, memory book, tree planting).

Realize that not talking about the loss doesn't make it go away.

Remember, what we resist, persists!

Encourage classmates to be a support system.

Recognize that laughter and play are a part of grieving.

Understand separation is the underlying pain of a grieving child.

Acknowledge that children often believe they have magical powers and need to create a reason for what has happened.

 Communicate with children by:

Using children's own language
Realizing children can talk about their experiences
Allowing children to ask their own questions
Creating honest discussion
Listening, watching, and waiting for the child to process his or her experience
Explaining to children the facts surrounding the loss

Resources for Children and a Dying Family Member

A Celebration of Life, a Journal for the Living (1997) by Paula Cellar and Janet Sieff. This is a journal to serve people during their dying process. It can also be used as a family activity to share memories, stories, and experiences.

A Journey Toward ... new hope ... preparing to say goodbye (1992) by Karen Robertson. This workbook is intended for children who are facing the impending death of someone they love.

Forever in My Heart (1992) by Jennifer Levine. This is a wonderful story for children to help them participate in life as a parent dies.

Just You and Me (1995) by Judy Richmond. A workbook designed to make memories with children, with ideas and activities for families facing terminal illness.

My Mom Is Dying (1994) by Jill McNamara. This is a child's diary about her mom's illness, dying, and death.

C H A P T E R   6

Especially for Educators

IDENTIFY CHILD • RECOGNIZE GRIEF AS A CRY FOR HELP
FIND RESOURCES • INSIST ON GETTING HELP

The Ball's in Your Court

We Can Make a Difference

Many educators are frustrated, overwhelmed, and drowning in accountability. Too often they lack immediate resources to help them pull a child through a period of crisis.

While waiting to present a seminar on loss and grief issues to elementary school counselors, one counselor confided a very interesting yet typical story.

Joey's mom had died when he was age seven. He was in second grade. An aunt reluctantly took him in. He began having severe attention-learning problems and acting-out behaviors after his mom's death. This is all too common after such a traumatic loss. In first grade, Joey had been a good student, achieving on grade level in reading and math. He was well liked by students and teachers. For the following two years he had no counseling or psychological help. His disruptive behaviors and ill performance in school were factors leading to his placement in a Level IV learning disabled class.

The counselor sadly relayed the story. She felt defeated that a child had fallen through the cracks of the educational system. Left on this path, he may very well be headed for the penal system next.

LIFE IS A PROCESS: LOSS · CHANGE · GROWTH

❝ *Two of the best kept secrets of the twentieth century are that everyone suffers and that suffering can be used for growth.* **❞**

Lawrence LeShan (Jackson, 1993)

Life is a process of loss, change, and growth. Understanding loss issues can make them more predictable and therefore less frightening. Through grief we can grow in inner and outer strength, and healing can take place.

EDUCATORS FACE LOSS ISSUES DAILY

Educators face loss issues every day with their job, the kids with whom they work, and the system in which they work. They may ask themselves these questions:

Will I get a raise?

Will I get the promotion?

Will I get my materials?

Will I lose my job?

Will I be accountable to parents, children, and administrators when I walk through the door?

Will I get the respect I need in the classroom today?

Will I achieve my learning with the children?

Will I be a victim of violence in the school?

CHILDREN FACE LOSS ISSUES DAILY

Kids face loss issues every day with teachers, other kids, and the system. They may ask themselves these questions:

Will I lose the baseball game?

Will my best friend like someone else?

Will the kids pick on me at lunch?

Will I fail a test?

Will I fail this grade?

Will I forget my homework?

Will my teacher like me?

Will I learn today?

Will my sick mother be OK when I'm at school?

Will they think I'm different because I go to speech class?

Will they make fun of my braces, my skin, my hair, my sex?

Will anyone discover my secrets? (Mom got drunk last night. Dad came into my bedroom. My brother got arrested by the police.)

BOBBY AND GREGORY'S STORIES: A CHILD'S VOICE IS HEARD

While working as a counselor in a school where the majority of children came from divorced and single parent homes, I met Bobby, a bright sixth grader. He had flourished under the love and support of his foster parents during the two years he had lived with them. They adored Bobby and Bobby adored them. Bobby and I would play chess in my room, and he would speak fondly of his natural mother, but spoke of his foster mother as "Mom."

One day the courts decided that Bobby would be better off going back to his natural mom. **No one asked him how he felt.** Bobby moved back. The devastation of that act wreaked havoc on the emotional and physical well being of both Bobby and his foster parents. Within a few months Bobby's grades dropped, his smile dimmed, and his natural mom began drinking again. No one had asked Bobby how he felt, and no one had offered a solution.

Many Bobbys have been, and still are, in the school system. One such Bobby, actually named Gregory, recently broke new ground by coming up with his own solution and making headlines in 1992.

Gregory contacted a lawyer on his own, and expressed his strong desire to terminate his parents' parental rights and divorce them. This was the first time a child had sued his parents on his own right. Usually an adult, guardian, or friend sues on behalf of the child. Gregory felt his mom and dad had abandoned and neglected him. He wanted the courts to consider children's choices in domestic matters and have children be "treated as people and not as property."

Gregory had found a permanent, stable home and wanted to stay there. His voice **needs to be heard** as part of the legal requirements in our courts. Kids need protection for their rights to participate in divorce and foster care decisions in the judicial system when the parental and governmental systems have not worked for them.

We Can See The Day Differently

We as educators need to identify the behaviors, thoughts, and feelings that grief and loss issues bring to the foreground. Our school day is an ongoing kaleidoscope of children working through their many grief processes.

Children "acting out" or "acting in" are crying for help. These behaviors may be a red flag to adults that a child is working through a grief issue.

We can create a SAFE and feeling environment for kids by turning humiliations into experiences that build self-esteem. So often grief issues have an immediate and direct effect of lowering self-esteem and creating guilt and shame, the underlying force behind many disruptive behaviors.

In encouraging children to talk about loss, we need to have the patience to wait before responding, and to think before we act. This lets us:

S - **Seize** the moment. Guide the child to give a good answer, rather than condemn a bad one.

A - **Act.** When in doubt, reach out. It works. Kids feel sincerity.

F - **Find** strengths. Every child has them. Children are taught to stuff feelings, and these feelings come out in other ways. If we really knew what was pushing that child to act out, we would never judge him.

E - **Establish** a relationship. Talk to the child alone. Let him or her know you are aware of his or her behaviors, and that you will be there if he or she needs to talk.

 Children will be more open to learning and relating if they are given avenues to express their bottled up feelings. Their academic, social, and spiritual growth will soar with the release of stored up hurts.

TEACHABLE MOMENTS

"Teachable moments" are an important concept for **unplanned** lessons. A teachable moment is a spontaneous mini-lesson inserted into the daily planned activities based on something that has just happened. Its **power** comes from catching the moment and creating a living, dynamic learning situation.

Teachable moments can be trauma related or a natural part of the day. It is important to seize these opportunities and not deny their value.

Mrs. Albert, a kindergarten teacher, confided her feelings of fear and inadequacy that held her back from relating in the here and now. Karen, a five-year-old, had recently experienced the death of her dad. Every time she mentioned Daddy, Mrs. Albert ignored her. This went on for three months. The teacher explained that she didn't know what to say, and so she avoided any mention of Dad in the classroom.

Sometimes we can integrate special vocabulary to help ease the flow of conversation. Open ended questions allow the child to remember and verbalize events and feelings. Mrs. Albert could have asked Karen, "What are some of the times you remember best with your Dad?" giving Karen an avenue for sharing. Had she asked a closed question such as, "Do you remember some good times with your Dad?" Karen could have easily just answered, "Yes."

Integrating a teachable moment into the classroom can be done easily if a class goldfish dies or if a dead worm is found after it rains. As educators, we can:

- Explain it is part of the life cycle,
- Have a funeral for it,
- Bury it,
- Talk about feelings,
- Make a class memory book or memory box,
- Read the books *"When Dinosaurs Die"* (Brown, 1996) or *"About Dying"* (Stein, 1974).

Hands-on practical curricula and manuals are available that provide lesson plans specific to each grade level.

An example of loss and grief lesson plans might be a first grade having a lesson on understanding the differences between dead and alive. Kids can examine live and dead plants, which could lead them into a discussion of the concept that when we die our bodies stop working. Many of these materials suggest readings such as *When Dinosaurs Die* (Brown, 1996) or *About Dying* (Stein, 1974) for young children.

In contrast, the fourth-grade lessons provide ideas to introduce discussion of loss and that it's OK to have your feelings. Suggested activities include speakers covering topics from losing a sports championship to a house being destroyed by a fire. Kids can brainstorm losses in groups and discuss them, collect newspaper articles on loss, or keep loss journals. *Charlotte's Web* (White, 1952) is a wonderful book to use with this age child. *The Hurt* by Teddi Doleski (1983) is a book for all ages that illustrates that the hurt grows when we hold onto it, and that "magic" can happen when we let it go. Resource corners in each classroom and in the school library benefit children of all ages.

A good example of integrating a trauma into a teachable moment is that of a caring fourth grade teacher. The children in her class were talking about nightmares and drawing pictures after hearing on the news about a seven-year-old girl who was brutally attacked by dogs. The class began writing the little girl and even collecting money for a music tape for her.

This teacher had chosen to transform the children's fear into a positive, empowering memory. Art Kirsch, educator and director of Detroit's "Kids In Crisis Program," emphasizes that these "emotional innoculations" of teachable moments are literally a shot in the arm for preparing children for their own next loss. Hopefully, the more comfortable we as educators become with these grief and loss issues, the more we can become role models for children to work through their grief. Through education, we can become increasingly aware of our own barriers and can conquer and dispel myths associated with grief.

Elementary, middle, and high school students and teachers can use spontaneous teachable moments as an opportunity for growth and learning. The mass murders by teens in Littleton, Colorado sent a wave of terror to kids, parents, and educators throughout our country and the world. This very poignant event shocked our nation, placing fear, sadness, and compassion in the hearts of many school children.

Thirteen-year-old Thomas called Mom at work, upset and scared. "I can't believe this is happening" as he watched the terrifying event on TV. I'm scared to go to school tomorrow, a lot of kids are staying home tomorrow, and I want to stay home too!"

Seven-year-old Mara watched the same news on TV and started to cry. "They are going to kill those kids the way they shot Tony (her fourteen-year-old-brother). She ran over to her grandmother, sat in her lap, began sucking her thumb and holding her tight. Fear, anxiety, and regression occur when events such as teen terrorism and murder in schools are in visible sight for all children to see. These visual imageries instill terror in children, and rekindle old wounds and regrieving.

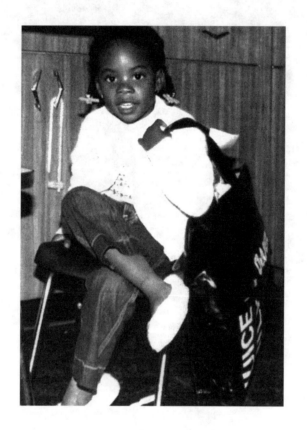

Class discussions and assignments can be incorporated into children's learning by using kids preoccupation with traumatic events or loss as a vehicle to release powerful feelings, reduce danger, and lesson anxiety. Allowing safe expression of powerful feelings can be a golden opportunity for educators to relate to students in a meaningful way.

Margaret, a third grader, was disappointed when she came to school that her teachers didn't even mention the killings at Columbine High School. She wanted to talk about it. "These murders are all that's on my mind," she thought. Alexander was glad his school chose to discuss the school shootings. The following is a summary of his class discussion led by his teacher, Mr. Harter, and the discussion questions asked:

> Do you feel safe at our school?
> What do you wish we would do to make school safe?
> What do you think about Columbine?
> Do you feel you understand what happened?
> Is there anything you don't understand?
> Would you like to do something to remember the students that died?

Students' reactions were open and varied. "This is so scary. This could happen to us!" Alice explained. "The news is always blaming violence on video games and music. What about the parents, the school, the politicians, gun control?" Joseph responded. Liam added, "I think Columbine is a real eye opener to everyone across the country to look out for each other and treat people with respect. The kids that murdered were reclusive—bullied a lot."

"What can we do to feel safe and change the violence?" asked Mr. Harter of his class. "Have gun detectors," Sara suggested. Melvin called out, "Have more police and security guards!" Tom said, "Stronger no-bully policies." And Joseph suggested "Let's just stay home from school." Mr. Harter felt teachers and principals could explain and institute a school policy on no violence and bullying with procedures for students to follow when an incident occurs. He warned, "If children hear a threat, "take any threat seriously. Any student who threatens another student's health or well being will be suspended or expelled. If you hear a threat you must notify an adult or you will be in jeopardy also."

The following was a poster that fourteen-year-old Liam made to represent his school's feelings of grief and commemorate the lives of all the students shot at Littleton. Every child in the entire school signed the poster.

 Sensitive life issues can be used in today's classrooms proactively to enhance student motivation by creating lessons that encourage kids to talk, write, or role-play complex daily situations.

Teachers can actively engage kids in a valuable assignment that allows expression and completes an educational task. A sensitive teacher allowed Christopher, a tenth-grade student who was grieving the death of four significant people in his life, to use an English assignment of poetry writing to express his deep feelings. The following is one of these poems about the sudden death of his friend Doug, followed by a heartfelt response by his teacher.

Doug Able (1999)

Christopher Hawk

You played a bold game of basketball,
Even though you were dizzy and wanted to fall.
You jumped high and shot well,
Which led us to victory at the sound of the bell.

We slapped five and bragged to the other team,
For the game had ended much like a dream.
We left the building and went to the parking lot.
And found the Caravan in the same spot.

We pulled out of the school and rolled over a bump,
A few seconds down the road I heard a large thump.
I turned around to see what fell,
And in the dark it was hard to tell.

I soon realized it was Doug draped over the seat.
I held him up and checked for a beat.
He looked through me as if I were a ghost,
He sat in his seat as motionless as a post.

He was a happy kid that didn't deserve to die.
For he was a friend on whom you could always rely.
He lived for soccer and tried his best,
Which is all you can ask from a kid now at rest.

His English teacher responded with the following note:

"These are well-written. I realize that comfort and well-meant words often
sound trite, but I offer them anyway. I truly admire your strength. I hope
writing these poems were a comfort to you as they were an enjoyment to me."

50/50 a+

Guidelines for Educational Referrals

Become familiar with local agencies and their programs. They can provide help for children and their families and connect them with community resources. When meeting with parents about the child,

1. present observations and concerns honestly to both parents if possible. Be clear, organized, and specific. Use a children's loss inventory as a resource. (A sample Children's Loss Inventory Checklist follows).

2. find out if the child is or was in counseling, and if the parents are familiar with specific community resources. (A sample list of community resources is provided in Chapter 8.)

3. offer to share information and observations with a person in the community of the parent's choice (clergy member, doctor, etc.).

4. maintain the privacy of the child. Only talk about the child with resource personnel in other agencies with the parent's permission.

5. obtain written authorization from a parent or guardian before releasing information. Protect the rights of the child and family. Date your request and specify the person in the agency to whom you are giving information.

6. suggest several possibilities for help to parents. Let them find the one that feels right to them.

7. let parents schedule the referral appointment.

8. suggest that the parents follow up with you after their first appointment.

9. ask the parent to keep you informed of any ways you can help the child during this period.

10. keep a list of significant dates (birth dates or date of loss) that may affect the child throughout school.

CHILDREN'S LOSS INVENTORY CHECKLIST: A COMPLETE PICTURE OF THE WHOLE CHILD

IDENTIFY CHILD

Name _____ Age_____ Grade_____

Address _____ Birthdate _____

Phone number _____ Today's date _____

REFERRAL INFORMATION

Reasons for referral _____

_____

Source for referral _____

IDENTIFY RECENT SIGNIFICANT LOSS

Relationship of deceased to child _____

What are the facts about the loss? (Who, what, where, how)

_____

_____

Who told the child? _____

How was he/she told? _____

Date of birth of deceased _____ Date of death of deceased _____

PREVIOUS LOSS AND GRIEF HISTORY

Include significant dates or birthdates involved in previous losses.

Divorce or separation _____ Date _____

Moving _____ Date _____

Friends Move Away _____ Date _____

Past Deaths_____Who?_____ Date _____

Pet Deaths_____Who?_____ Date _____

Parents Changing Job_____ Date _____

Parents Losing Job_____ Date _____

Fire _____ Robbery_____ Date_____

Other_____ Date_____

INHERITED FAMILY LOSS

Examples are a grandfather killed in a war or a previous sibling death

_____

_____

FAMILY UNIT

Single parent _____ Divorce_____

Unmarried _____ Adoption_____

Natural parents _____ Blended family_____

FAMILY HISTORY OF CHRONIC CULTURAL LOSS

Drugs_____ Injuries _____

Crime _____ Unemployment _____

MEDICAL HISTORY

Significant parent illness _____

Significant children's illness _____

PREVIOUS SCHOOL HISTORY

Grades_____

Progress_____

Participation_____

ASSESSMENT HISTORY

Standardized tests _____ Date _____

_____

Speech and language evaluation _____ Date _____

_____

Educational assessment _____ Date _____

_____

Psychological evaluation _____ Date _____

_____

IDENTIFY CHILD'S ATTITUDE TOWARDS SIGNIFICANT OTHERS

Siblings _____

_____

Parents _____

_____

Friends _____

_____

Pets _____

_____

Self _____

IDENTIFY LIKES AND DISLIKES

Interests _____

Likes _____

Dislikes_____

Abilities _____

    Likes _____

    Dislikes _____

IDENTIFY PRESENT BEHAVIORS AT SCHOOL
(Check those that apply)

Disruptive in school _____ Failing grades _____

Inability to concentrate _____ Increased absenteeism _____

Fighting with peers _____ Withdrawn _____

Using bad language _____ Very tired _____

Physical complaints (headaches, stomachaches) _____

Nervousness _____ Other _____

IDENTIFY PRESENT BEHAVIORS AT HOME
(Check those that apply)

Less interaction _____ Sleeplessness _____

Poor eating _____ Bedwetting _____

Clinging to parents _____ Nightmares _____

Increased perfectionism _____ Crying _____

Talks excessively about loss _____

Fighting with siblings or parents _____

Fear of dark, noise, or robbers _____

IDENTIFY PRESENT PEER BEHAVIORS
(Check those that apply)

More arguing _____

Less interest in play dates _____

Less communication with peers _____

Others_____

_____

RECOMMENDATIONS

Team conference _____

In-school individual counseling _____

In-school peer group counseling _____

Referral to counseling agency _____

Referral to support group _____

Testing _____

FOLLOW UP

Monthly follow-up _____ Source _____ Date_____

Information_____

_____

PROFESSIONAL HELP

When any of the following are observed in a child, professional intervention may be helpful.

1. Child continually refuses to share thoughts or feelings about loss. *Tommy doesn't cry or talk about his mom's recent death.*

2. Child is extremely clingy to adults. *Tommy screams and cries. He is afraid to go to school and wants to stay home.*

3. Child has been lied to about loss. *Tommy was told his dad died of a heart attack. He overheard his dad had committed suicide.*

4. Child threatens to hurt him or her self. *Tommy tells his best friend that he wants to kill himself.*

5. Child won't socialize. *Tommy quits baseball, soccer, or riding bikes.*

6. Child becomes involved in drugs or alcohol. *Tommy's mom finds marijuana in his room.*

7. Child is cruel to animals or physically abusive to other children. *Tommy repeatedly kicks his dog and throws sticks at him.*

8. Child has had a very difficult relationship to the deceased. *Tommy's deceased dad was an alcoholic who physically abused him.*

9. Child shows extremes in not sleeping or eating. *Tommy has lost 10 pounds in three weeks. He wakes up crying at 2 a.m.*

10. Child is failing school. *Tommy got 4 F's and 5 N's on his report card.*

11. Child exhibits sudden unexplained change. *Tommy gets suspended from school for continually staring fights with other children.*

 Children exhibit normal signs of loss and grief in many ways. It is the *extreme behaviors* and *intensity of feelings and actions* that signal that outside intervention is needed.

Suggestions for Parents Seeking Professional Help

If parents are seeking professional help for their child, you may want to recommend they:

1. **Use** word-of-mouth recommendations as a source of referrals. These referrals can be made by a friend, physician, or guidance counselor.

2. **Seek** out professional mental health associations, such as social work, psychology, or counseling associations, that provide listings and referrals for loss and grief therapists.

3. **Meet** with the therapist if possible to decide if he or she is right for their child. Counselors or therapists typically work with children using play therapy tools such as art, music, clay, and storytelling as well as dialogue to facilitate the expression of feeling.

4. **Ask** questions of the counselors or threrapists.

   How does he or she approach loss and grief issues?

   How long are sessions?

   What is the cost per session?

   How frequently are the parents informed about or included in sessions?

   What are the limits of confidentiality?

 Confidentiality is an important component of child therapy. If the child has been abused or has thoughts of hurting him or herself or others, the parent needs to know. Otherwise, the parent needs to understand the therapist-child relationship is separate and unique. The child's thoughts and feelings need to remain private. Then parent and child both gain a sense of respect for this valued relationship.

We Can Make a Difference

TO BEGIN, WE CAN

1. Identify the child who is dealing with a specific, significant loss.

2. Recognize the grief and loss issue he or she is working through.

3. Realize his or her behaviors are "a cry for help." These behaviors are threatening to the system, yet they can be turned around if identified early.

4. Insist on getting help. How can a child learn in school and enjoy his or her day productively when he or she is carrying overwhelming feelings of grief?

5. Find resources: community, agencies, staff, peers.

6. Use team conferences as a checks and balances system to safeguard a child's "right" to emotional as well as intellectual help.

7. Develop an intra-school database where counselors can connect children within the same school with specific problems to each other in peer groups.

8. Create an inter-school database to connect children in different schools together when none exist within their own schools.

9. Reassure teachers that educators can help. A panicked teacher can't create the environment a child needs to work through the hurt.

10. See the child differently. Expand time. Wait ten extra seconds to talk. Talk less. Be with him or her more. Let children tell you where they are, and what they need. Have faith in them. Trust their perceptions. They are the only ones that really understand what they are going through. Let them explore and express freely.

Resources for Educators

Cassini, Jacqueline and L. Rogers (1990). *Death and the Classroom*. A teacher's textbook that confronts death in the classroom.

Dudley, John (1995). *When Grief Comes to Schools*. School districts are encouraged to use this book to establish and prepare crisis teams in the event of a tragedy.

Gliko-Braden, Majel (1992). *Grief Comes to Class*. This book is meant to help teachers and parents assist bereaved children.

Goldman, Linda (1996). *Breaking the Silence: A Guide to Help Children with Complicated Grief Suicide, Homicide, AIDS, Violence, and Abuse*. A helpful resource guide for parents and professionals to help children with complicated grief issues.

Goldman, Linda (2000). *Helping the Grieving Child in the Classroom*. A practical guide to help grieving children after initial loss and continuing throughout their school career.

McEvoy, Alan (1992). *When Disaster Strikes*. This small book prepares educators for bus accidents, murders, suicides, tornados, and other community catasrophes.

Miller, Karen (1996). *The Crisis Manual*. A good manual for early childhood teachers to help handle difficult problems such as community violence, death, divorce, AIDS, and abuse.

Stevenson, Robert (1994). *What Will We Do? Preparing a School Community to Cope With Crisis*. This clear and informative book helps prepare school personnel to help children cope with death-related topics.

The Dougy Center (1998). *Helping the Grieving Student: A Guide for Teachers*. A guide for teachers to help children through their grief processes.

C H A P T E R   7

The Community Grief Team

THE GUIDANCE COUNSELOR • THE COACH

THE TEACHER • AUNTS, UNCLES, COUSINS • THE POLICE

THE PRINCIPAL • THE CLERGY • THE BABYSITTER

❝ There are two things we can hope to give our children One of these is roots; the other, wings. ❞

Hodding Carter, III

Where Do We Go from Here?

This is a question that needs to be addressed for all of the grieving children in the world during this millenium. We have gained a basic understanding of the child and his or her grief process, and now we need to ask ourselves the question, "How can we implement these understandings into today's world?" The phrase, "It takes a village to raise a child" has become a very popular one. I have found that it takes a village, a community, a nation, and a world to care for and support our grieving children.

The more we as parents, educators, therapists, and other caring professionals can join together in creating a cohesive unit, sharing similar thought forms, supports, resources, and information—the more congruent a child's grieving experience becomes.

Imagine a child's journey through grief as a three dimensional hologram, where each and every part is as important and representative as the whole. The teacher, the doctor, the baby sitter, the guidance counselor, the friend, the clergy, the aunt and uncle, the cousins, the therapist all become a team of like-minded adults and children offering congruency in a world of loss.

Usually when children grieve, their world feels fragmented. The more consistency we can create throughout their lives, the more solid and secure their world will become. Our goal is to create a Community Grief Team to meet the needs of our grieving youth.

As we join together as a united group, we allow each member to become an advocate, educator, liaison, therapist, and friend working in support and recognition of the grieving child. Throughout the home, the school, the community, and the nation, there are support people and organizations available to facilitate the following five tasks of a community grief team.

TASK 1: WORKING WITH THE SURVIVING PARENT OR GUARDIAN

EDUCATING CARING ADULTS

- Educate caring adults on the common signs and symptoms of children's grief.
- Create age-appropriate words to use to open dialogue and grieve freely.
- Identify unresolved grief of the caring adult so it is not unknowingly projected onto children.

The community grief team first works with the surviving parent or guardian to help create words to use with the children. So often caring adults need to understand what the common signs of grief are and how to approach them in order to reduce anxieties that unconsciously get projected onto the children.

Dave was a six-year-old whose Mom had suffered with deep depression all of her life. She shot and killed herself in her bedroom closet, leaving Dave, his ten-year old sister, Ellen, and their dad to find her. Dad called me as a grief therapist to "nip any problems in the bud," before any adverse reactions could develop. Dave's dad needed to be educated in the tremendous impact the death of a parent has on a child, and the added shame and shock of such a sudden and brutal death. His awareness needed to be expanded in knowing that grief is a long and ongoing process and cannot be halted or diminished in a few therapy sessions.

When Dave's guidance counselor visited his home after his mom's funeral, he ran up to her, grabbed her hand, and explained "My mom shot herself in the head in her closet in the bedroom. You want to see?" leading her into the room. He repeated this with many of the visitors that came that day. This preschooler needed to tell his story over and over again—a common sign of grief in children. As the counselor sat down to read Dave and his sister a story about a mom that dies, he jumped up and said:

" I don't want to talk about this anymore. It's making me really really sad—I want to play! "

He ran out of the room. He needed to play, often a way young children respond and work through their grief. Ellen responded to the story quite differently, agreeing with the child in the story about some feelings of happiness.

" *I'm happy like that little girl. That's how I feel. I feel happy. But my dad makes me feel guilty about being happy. He thinks I should be sad, be crying. Sad is a bad feeling because my mom is where she wanted to be. This is what she wanted. If she's happy, I'm happy.* **"**

Ellen had lived most of her young life in a suicide watch over mom, constantly feeling her job was to make her mother happy and rarely succeeding. This overwhelming burden may have been relieved by her mom's death, ending the pressure she had explained to her counselor of "doing the job of keeping her mother happy." It is normal for children to feel a sense of relief of being freed from this complicated situation. Dad had attempted to prescribe how Ellen should feel, instead of respecting the dignity of her grieving process.

 Parents often don't understand the tremendous impact of their unresolved grief on the child and the secondary loss of parental trust that can arise.

Tom was a fourteen-year-old whose dad committed suicide on Tom's birthday. Filled with shame, he stopped calling his old friends, fearing if he called them he would have to tell them that his dad died, and then he would have to tell how his dad died. Tom often said his mom was always worried he was lying to her, doing drugs and alcohol, or getting into trouble with the law. One year later, Mom called and shared for the first time that her husband had left a suicide note which read:

Dear Margaret,

It is your fault I am killing myself. Do not tell Thomas how I died, and remember to keep and eye on Thomas because you know—suicide runs in our family!!!

> *Love,*
> *Henry*

This mom's unacknowledged terror and guilt was unknowingly projected onto her son, creating a huge anxiety for him because not only had he lost his dad and his friends, but also his mother's trust. Had this mom been educated in the signs of complicated grief, she could have illuminated some of the devastation her child experienced.

Resources for Parents to Read with Children:

Bart Speaks Out on Suicide by Linda Goldman (1998). This book is an interactive story for young children on suicide, told by a terrier named Bart. It provides words to use with suicide. It also allows the child to identify and express thoughts and feelings about their person that died as well as how that person died.

TASK 2: PROVIDING A SCHOOL ADVOCATE FOR THE GRIEVING CHILD

The community grief team provides an advocate for the grieving child in the school system. This advocate makes sure the following practices will be implemented by the teacher or counselor when the child comes back to school after a death and allows the child to be a part of the decision making process. These practices remain a part of the child's grief experience throughout the year and are continued for the next year if it is necessary.

ADVOCACY FOR THE GRIEVING CHILD

- Permit the child to leave the room if needed without explanation.
- Suggest the child choose a designated adult to talk with.
- Choose designated place to go within school as a safe space.
- Allow the child to call home.
- Invite child to visit the school nurse as a reality check.
- Assign a class helper.
- Create private teacher time.
- Give child more academic progress reports.
- Modify some work assignments.
- Inform faculty, PTA, parents, and children of loss.

Charlie was a sixth grader who was a star athlete for the intramural basketball game. Many of the parents had gathered to watch their children play. Coach Matt went up to Charlie before the game and asked, "Is your dad here today?" "No," Charlie grumbled. "He had to work." Charlie played his worst game. Coach Matt was unaware that Charlie's dad had died a year ago, and there was no written record to communicate this in the school.

Had this school system had an established practice of using a loss inventory, this lapse in communication may not have had such a devastating impact on Charlie.

Jesse was a seven-year-old boy whose mom died after a long and debilitating bout with cancer. Mother's Day was two weeks after Mom's death. While kids made Mother's Day cards someone came to get Jesse out of the room. No one offered the teacher or Jesse the insight to invite him to make a symbolic card for his mom or maybe one for his grandmother instead. This grieving child was made to feel different and isolated by being removed from the class.

Mrs. Morgan, Jesse's teacher gave an assignment for all the children, "Interview your mom with Mother's Day questions." Jesse came home hysterical. He was terrified his teacher would be furious because he couldn't interview Mom. That same week the PTA sent a note home with Jesse with this message:

> *Dear Jesse,*
>
> *Please give this note to your mom and thank her for her help in the PTA.*
>
> *MRS. SMITH/PTA PRESIDENT*

Jesse wept uncontrollably when he read it.

Lack of communication and lack of a central focus that guarantees everyone in the system has an awareness of this death is apparent. Certainly, the PTA did not want to hurt this child, but their miscommunication was devastating.

TASK 3: PROVIDE TRAININGS

TRAININGS

- Children's social living units and guidance curriculums
- Faculty meetings and PTA workshops
- Schools and universities that train caring professionals
- Staff in-service workshops and seminars at workplace

The community grief team must provide trainings for all parents, educators, therapists, physicians, clergy, and other caring professionals on ways to work with children and grief. Many times, the old paradigms about children and grief within the therapeutic community still resurface. A mental health professional once explained "Everything is loss and grief, we already know this." Each day more and more unique children's grief issues emerge. The enormity of information and resources becoming available on this subject is astounding and a continuing source of learning and growth for the professional.

A recent article offering advice to parents of grieving children shocked me. The advice explained how to cure your kids from talking about death. The giver of this advice felt his own child was asking too many questions about death. He explained a new program for his son. "You are only allowed to ask two questions about death. If you ask a third, that means you need to calm yourself down. To help you calm down you will need to go to your room for 30 minutes." The article explained the child was "cured" within a month.

This advice in a well respected public media resource may leave many well-meaning, searching parents feeling confused and misguided. Information like this can potentially shut down the very process we want to bring out into the open.

We can't "cure" grief. We can only support healing after a loss by facilitating its safe expression.

We need to encourage PTAs to provide workshops for parents preventatively, and when a crisis arises. This allows parents to work through their own fears and feelings when their child experiences a loss, and offers words to use and a perspective on grief that can be shared with their children.

School systems and other professional workplaces can provide trainings and in-service courses for all personnel. These trainings heighten awareness of and sensitivity to the normal and complicated signs of children's grief by enhancing ways to approach and work with the children in their system.

Colleges and universities can implement undergraduate and graduate courses to train future educators, therapists, physicians, clergy, and all other caring professionals in unique, yet universal ways to work with grieving children. This will prepare professionals for future events they will surely face.

TASK 4: PROVIDE PREVENTATIVE AND CRISIS EDUCATION FOR CHILDREN

EDUCATE CHILDREN

- Teachable moments
- Guidance curricula
- Life issues units
- Grief support groups

Children in grief need the support of their peers, for they tend to hide their grief or withdraw from friendships because they feel different. Eight-year-old Sara's mom died of a sudden heart attack. Six months later, while getting her hair cut, the beautician unknowingly asked her where he mom was that day. "She's home," Sara replied. Wanting to feel like all the other kids she know, she said her mom was waiting for her at home. Sara hated feeling different, and yearned to be like the other kids

"I'm not going to tell anyone how much I miss my mother," she explained. "You can tell me." I replied.

Sara needed to be educated in the common signs of grief. She needed to know that most kids feel different when a parent dies and that this feeling is common and can be shared. She and other children can benefit from school systems that provide support groups within the school as a base to share with peers similar experiences. Children can make use of the internet to provide inter- and intraschool groups to communicate and maintain peer support. Private chat rooms can be formed to maintain confidentiality.

Schools can also educate the children by creating a loss and grief school curriculum that provides preventive information, educational interventions, crisis interventions, and follow-ups for the grieving child throughout his or her school career. This can be incorporated into life issues curricula, guidance curricula, and trainings that help find teachable moments.

The following poem was written by a child, 11-year-old Michelle, as a way of expressing her special and intimate feelings of missing her mom.

My Special Person

My Special Person is gone,
- I know she's never coming back
She's the brightest star that glows
- And the main bird that flys.
We all miss her, but we know
. she's with us all
So don't stand at her grave & cry,
She is not there, she did not die.

Michelle
Age 10

TASK 5: CREATE A RESPECT FOR OUR MULTICULTURAL WORLD

MULTICULTURAL ADAPTATION

- honor specific rituals and customs particular to ethnic groups
- develop ways to use second language in griefwork
- respect the unique belief system of specific culture

Jose was an eight-year-old boy who came to see me one year after his dad, Juan, had capsized his boat while sailing and plunged suddenly to his death. Mom and Jose were shocked and devastated, and this first year was a nightmare and blur. Maria spoke not only of the death of her husband, but the loss of her rich culture. They spoke Spanish at home, and after Juan died, Jose did not and could not carry on this second language.

Maria yearned for Spanish speaking people to relate to, and a way to pass this heritage onto her son. We located a Spanish speaking support group, and a memory book for grieving children in Spanish. This book allowed Jose to feel closer to his dad, and more eager to learn the language and the traditions of his culture. Written grief resources translated into other languages are valuable resources for children and families in highly ethnic areas.

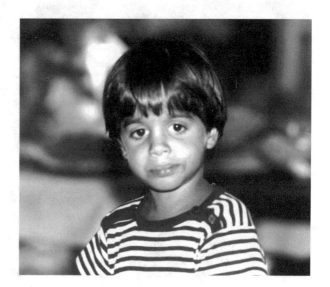

Multicultural Resources

Annie and the Old One (1971) by Misha Miles. This beautiful story illustrates the Native American belief system that one chooses their time to die. Ages 6-10.

The Day of the Dead (1993) by George Ancoma. This book helps create an understanding of the rituals used for the Mexican celebration of the Day of the Dead. Ages 6-11.

Los Recuerdos Viven Eternamente (1997) by Sharon Rugg. A memory book for children written in English and Spanish that allows the children to use another language and retain their cultural heritage. Ages 5-10.

Barley and Eve Sitting Shiva (1995) by Karen Carney. A wonderful story told through the eyes of dogs, which creates for young children an understanding of the Jewish rituals involved in the period of mourning. Ages 3-7.

The Community Grief Team: What Can We Do?

Laying the framework for a community grief team is the first step towards action. The development of life issues, curricula, and guidance and social living programs is essential. These trainings and curricula include prevention, intervention, and postvention techniques for children, parents, educators, and other caring professionals on issues children experience in today's world. They emphasize resources that match the needs of the grieving child, from birth through the school career, and highlight accountability for loss and grief issues that may greatly impair learning and emotional well-being if not addressed openly.

The next step is to create a broad based mission statement that will outline the emergence of a community based children's grief team. This mission statement includes areas of focus on trainings, materials, resources, and supports for children, parents, and professionals within the home, school, community, nation, and world.

MISSION STATEMENT

The goal of the Community Grief Team is to create a broad based program to meet the emotional, social, educational, and spiritual needs of the population of children with loss and grief issues.

Loss and grief issues range from death due to violence or suicide, and loss due to sudden trauma, chronic illness, divorce, AIDS, teen pregnancy, imprisonment, alcoholism, drugs, and many other causes. This community grief team focuses on the creation and maintenance of six separate components under the umbrella of education and mental health (see page 154).

I have been working with children and families for many years. Twenty years were spent as an elementary school teacher and guidance counselor in the public school system. Serving as a liaison to children, teachers, and administrators was coupled with being chairman of The School Team, a school based group used to identify and create learning strategies for children.

This strong educational background, combined with my present experience as a certified grief therapist and certified grief educator, allows me to see that many problems identified as "learning disabled," "attention deficit," or just "slow learning" had a direct relationship to emotional well-being and, more specifically, to unresolved grief and trauma.

Experience as a classroom teacher and guidance counselor coupled with therapeutic under-standings have profoundly affected my perception of these problems as being anything but iso-lated, fragmented, and unrelated. In fact, they appear to be a very congruent continuum.

Children with grief and loss issues often manifest the same behavioral signs used to diagnose ADD and LD—impulsivity, distractability, and hyperactivity. Often kids are misdiagnosed, leaving them in a learning disabled tract that may provide Ritalin or other medications for behavior control and convenience rather than address the underlying issues.

These children need to be seen through a different vision—that of a normal child living and working through many emotional life issues. A new concept of "normal" and "normal learning" must be put into place to meet the needs of today's and tomorrow's kids. They are capable of productive lives and successful learning, but may be temporarily stuck in blocks of time. If not addressed, children remain permanently locked into silence and repression, and the cost to their own lives and society is immeasurable.

COMPONENTS OF THE COMMUNITY GRIEF TEAM

1. **Intervention**: preventional, educational, and crisis
2. **Information and resources**: books, articles, data, community and national agencies and programs
3. **Trainings**: parents, children, educators, therapists, clergy, physicians, other caring pro-fessionals
4. **Supports**: children, parents, professionals
5. **Curricula**: life issues—guidance and social living programs, health related studies
6. **Research**: children, grief, learning, esteem

Many of these components are presently available and in use in some schools. Now we need an appropriate integration—a new and shared paradigm, for the parental, educational, psychological, health-related, and spiritual communities.

A shared vision of learning, emotional and physical well-being, and personal growth is essential. A child that becomes a burden on the community may also be disowned by family, friends, and schools, and then relegated solely to the psychological community. Learning strategies, emotional needs, and community resources must merge as a congruent unit for the common interest and healing of the grieving child.

 People of like minds must join together and produce a working model for parents, educators, mental health professionals, and community agencies that meets the emotional, social, and spiritual needs of the children as well as their academic needs. By meeting these needs we can enhance their capacity to learn and grow as human beings.

Community and National Resources Point the Way to Help

COMMUNITY RESOURCES FOR CHILDREN'S GRIEF AND LOSS ISSUES

- Mental health agencies
- Funeral service professionals
- Clergy
- School psychologists
- Nurses
- Local support groups for children and families
- Agencies or programs dealing with specific losses
- Hotlines

- Hospice programs
- Pediatricians
- School counselors
- Student personnel workers
- Grief camps

National Resources and Organizations

AMERICAN ASSOCIATION OF SUICIDOLOGY (AAS)
4201 Connecticut Ave.
Suite 310
Washington, DC 20008
202-237-2280

ASSOCIATION FOR THE CARE OF CHILDREN'S HEALTH
7910 Woodmont Ave.
Bethesda, MD 20814
301-654-6549

ASSOCIATION FOR DEATH EDUCATION AND COUNSELING (ADEC)
432 North Main St.
West Hartford, CT 06117-2507
860-586-7503

BATON ROUGE CRISIS INTERVENTION CENTER
4837 Revere Ave.
Baton Rouge, LA 70808
504-924-1431

CENTER FOR LOSS AND GRIEF THERAPY
10400 Connecticut Ave.
Suite 514
Kensington, MD 20985
301-942-6440

CENTER FOR LOSS AND LIFE TRANSITIONS
3735 Broken Arrow Rd.
Fort Collin, CO 80526
303-226-6050

CHILDREN'S DEFENSE FUND
25 E St. NW
Washington, DC 20001-0500
202-628-8787

CHILDREN'S HOSPICE INTERNATIONAL
11011 King St.
Suite 131
Alexandria, VA 22314
703-556-042

COMPASSIONATE FRIENDS INC.
National Headquarters
PO Box 1347
Oak Brook, IL 60521
312-323-5010

THE COVE: A SUPPORT PROGRAM FOR GRIEVING CHILDREN & FAMILIES
New England Center for Loss & Transition
PO Box 292
Guilford, CT 06437
203-456-1734

D'ESOPO RESOURCE CENTER
280 Main St.
Wethersfield, CT 06109
860-563-5677

DOUGY CENTER
P.O. Box 86852
Portland, OR 97286
503-775-5683

DOWN'S SYNDROME SOCIETY
666 Broadway, Suite 810
New York, NY 10012
800-221-2402

ELE'S PLACE
600 W. St. Joseph St., Suite 1-G
Lansing, MI 48933
517-482-1315

GOOD GRIEF PROGRAM
Judge Baker Guidance Center
295 Longwood Ave.
Boston, MA 02115
617-232-8390

HOPE FOR BEREAVED, INC.
(Support Groups and Telephone Help)
4500 Onondaga Blvd.
Syracuse, NY 13219
315-475-4673

HOSPICE EDUCATION INSTITUTE
P.O. Box 713
Essex, Connecticut 06426-0713
800-331-1620 (Computerized Hospice Link)

INNER SOURCE
980 Awald Dr.
Annapolis, MD 21403
410-269-6298

INSTITUTE FOR THE ADVANCEMENT OF SERVICE
111 S. Columbus St.
Old Towne, VA 22320
703-706-5333

KIDSPEACE NATIONAL CENTER FOR KIDS IN CRISIS
1650 Broadway
Bethlehem, PA 18015-3998
1-800-8KID-123

KIDS AND CRISIS
PO Box 3201
Center Lane, MI 48015
810-557-6089

KID'S PLACE
PO Box 258
Edmond, OK 73083
405-348-6777

MOTHER'S AGAINST DRUNK DRIVING (MADD)
669 Airport Freeway, Suite 310
Hurst, TX 76053
800-633-6233

NATIONAL ASSOCIATION FOR CHILDREN WITH AIDS
P.O. Box 15485
Durham, NC 27704
919-477-5288

NATIONAL HOSPICE ORGANIZATION
1901 N. Ft. Myer Dr.
Arlington, VA 22209
703-243-5900

NATIONAL SUDDEN INFANT DEATH SYNDROME FOUNDATION
105000 Little Patuxent Parkway, Suite 420
Columbia, MD 21044
800-221-SIDS

NEW ENGLAND CENTER FOR LOSS AND TRANSITION
PO Box 292
Guilford CT 06437-0292
800-887-5677

PARENTS OF MURDERED CHILDREN
1739 Bella Vista
Cincinnati, OH 45237
513-721-LOVE

PARENTS WITHOUT PARTNERS
7910 Woodmont Ave., Suite 1000
Bethesda, MD 20814
800-638-8078

PARENTS CAMPAIGN FOR HANDICAPPED CHILDREN AND YOUTH
Closer Look
Box 1492
Washington, DC 20013
202-822-7900

PREGANCY AND INFANT LOSS CENTER
1421 E. Wayzata Blvd., Suite 30
Wayzata, MN 55391
612-473-9372

RESOLVE THRU SHARING
LaCrosse Lutheran Hospital/Gundersen
   Clinic, Ltd.
1910 South Ave.
LaCrosse, WI 54601
608-791-4747

RONALD McDONALD HOUSE
419 East 86th St.
New York, NY 10028
212-876-1590

SHARE/PERINATAL NETWORK
St. Elizabeth's Hospital
211 South Third St.
Belleville, IL 62222
314-947-6164

SUICIDE PREVENTION CENTER
5417 Sherier Place N.W.
Washington, DC 20016
202-365-85

SURVIVORS OF SUICIDE
Suicide Prevention Center
184 Salem Ave.
Dayton, OH 45406
513-223-9096

Community Resources and Support Groups

The following resources and supports are examples of what is available in local communities.

ADVOCATES FOR CHILDREN AND YOUTH, INC.
300 Cathedral St., Suite 500
Baltimore, MD 21201
410-547-9200

CALVERT HOSPICE
(Kid's Bereavement Groups)
PO Box 838
Prince Frederick, MD 20678
410-535-0892

CARDINAL SHEEHAN CENTER— STELLA MARIS HOSPICE
("Me Too!" Children's Bereavement Program)
2300 Dulaney Valley Rd.
Towson, MD 21204
410-252-4500 EXT. 287

CHILDREN OF SEPARATION & DIVORCE, INC.
2000 Century Plaza #121
Columbia, MD 21044
410-740-9553

CHILDREN'S HOME HEALTH CARE
111 Michigan Ave., N.W.
Washington, DC 20010
202-939-4663

FAMILY SUPPORT CENTER/(KID'S BEREAVEMENT GROUPS)
4308 Montgomery Ave.
Bethesda, MD 20814
301-718-2467

GRIEF CRISIS PROGRAM
Fairfax County
8348 Traford Lane, Suite 400
Springfield, VA 22152
703-866-2100

HOWARD COUNTY SEXUAL ASSAULT CENTER
Gorman Plaza Building (Kid's Support Groups)
8950 Route 108, Suite 124
Columbia, MD 21045
410-964-0504

HOSPICE OF NORTHERN VA
6400 Arlington Blvd., Suite 1000
Falls Church, VA 22042
703-534-7070

JUST FOR KIDS THE FAMILY LIFE CENTER (KID'S SUPPORT GROUP FOR HOMES WITH DRUGS AND ALCOHOL)
10451 Twin Rivers Rd.
Columbia, MD 21044
410-997-3557

THE MARYLAND COMMITTEE FOR CHILDREN

608 Water St.
Baltimore, MD 21202
410-752-7588

MEDICAL ILLNESS COUNSELING CENTER

Chevy Chase Metro Building
Suite 530
Two Wisconsin Circle
Chevy Chase, MD 20815
301-654-3638

MONTGOMERY COUNTY HOSPICE/ (CHILDREN'S BEREAVEMENT GROUPS)

1450 Research Blvd.
Rockville, MD 20850
301-279-2566

"MY FRIEND'S HOUSE" (SUPPORT GROUPS FOR KIDS)

Fairfax Hospital/Life with Cancer
3300 Gallows Rd.
Falls Church, VA 22046
703-698-2841

PARENT ENCOURAGEMENT CENTER

10100 Connecticut Ave.
Kensington, MD 20895
301-929-8824

ST. FRANCIS CENTER

5135 Macarthur Blvd. N.W.
Washington, DC 20016
202-365-8500

Grief Camps for Children

CAMP COMFORT
(SPONSORED BY THE KID'S PLACE)
PO Box 258, Dept. ES
Edmond, OK 73083
405-348-6777

CAMP JAMIE
(SPONSORED BY THE HOSPICE OF
**   FREDERICK COUNTY)**
Division of Federick Memorial Healthcare
PO Box 1799
Frederick, MD 21702
301-698-3030

CAMP NEW HOPE
(SPONSORED BY DELAWARE HOSPICE)
911 S. Dupont Highway
Dover, DE
800-838-9800

KATERPILLAR KIDS
(sponsored by Medcenter Hospice)
9241-B Park West Blvd.
Knoxville, TN 32923
423-541-1738

Hotlines

CHILD ABUSE HOTLINE	800-4ACHILD
GRIEF RECOVERY HOTLINE	800-445-4808
KID SAVE	800-543-7283
NATIONAL AIDS HOTLINE	800-342-AIDS
NATIONAL CENTER FOR MISSING & EXPLOITED CHILDREN	800-843-5678
NATIONAL COALITION AGAINST DOMESTIC VIOLENCE	800-333-7233
NATIONAL RUNAWAY AND SUICIDE HOTLINE	800-621-4000
PARENT'S ANONYMOUS	800-421-0352

CHAPTER 9

Let's Explore Materials

- BOOKS
- VIDEOS
- MANUALS
- GUIDES
- CURRICULUMS
- CD-ROMS
- WEBSITES

There is Something for Every Loss

Today's Materials—
A Twenty-First
Century Update

As parents and professionals, we are not alone. Many new and useful materials are available for parents, educators, therapists, other child caregivers, and even children. These materials provide practical resources and information that can be used, as well as state of the art literature for the millennium covering the spectrum of topics of grief and loss issue for children.

These materials are geared to different ages and different developmental levels, and often stress that ideas designed to prepare and help children through inevitable loss must be age-appropriate.

Annotated Bibliography

BOOKS FOR ADULTS

Bertman, Sandra (1999). *Grief and Healing Arts*. Amityville, NY. Baywood Publishing Co. Inc. A well done book showing ways to use healing arts through grief.

Bothum, Linda. (1988). *When Friends Ask About Adoption*. Chevy Chase, MD: Swan Pub. A useful question and answer guide on adoption.

Burt, Sandy and Linda Perlis. (1999). *Parents as Mentors*. Rocklin, CA: Proma. A new perspective on parents as a child's first mentor.

Coles, Robert. (1991). *The Spiritual Life of Children*. Boston, MA: Houghton Mifflin Co. A book that reflects the inner world of children.

DeSpelder, Lynne & Albert Strickland (1999). *The Last Dance: Encountering Death & Dying*. Mountain View, CA: Mayfield Publishing Co. This book presents a comprehensive and readable introduction to the study of death and dying.

Edwards, Tess and Mary Derouard. (1995). *Hope in Healing*. Ontario, Canada: Source Re-Source. A useful guide for survivors of sexual abuse.

Fitzgerald, Helen. (1992). *The Grieving Child*. New York, NY: Simon & Schuster. A wonderful guide for parents to work with children's grief.

Fitzgerald, Helen. (1994). *The Mourning Handbook*. New York, NY: Simon & Schuster. A thorough and practical resource for families.

Fox, Sandra. (1988). *Good Grief: Helping Groups of Children When a Friend Dies*. Boston, MA: New England Association for the Education of Young Children. An excellent source of information for adults working with children whose friends have died.

Frankel, Fred. (1996). *Good Friends Are Hard to Find: Help Your Child Find, Make, and Keep Friends*. Pasadena, CA: Perspective. This book helps parents help children find and make friends and work with issues like teasing, bullying, and difficult relationships.

Frankl, Victor. (1984). *Man's Search for Meaning*. New York, NY: Simon and Schuster. A powerful account of the author's imprisonment in Nazi Germany and the love that helped him survive his losses.

Furth, Gregg. (1988). *The Secret World of Drawings*. Boston, MA: Sigo Press. A comprehensive look at children's artwork and ways of understanding it.

Gardner, Howard. (1993). *Frames of Mind: The Theory of Multiple Intelligences*. New York, NY: Basic Books. Gardner's theory and practical application for school systems is a fresh look at the way children learn.

Gil, Eliana. (1991). *The Healing Power of Play*. New York, NY: Guilford. This book gives a history of play therapy and specific considerations for working with abused and neglected children.

Golden, Tom, (1994) *Swallowed by a Snake*. Gaithersburg, MD: Golden Healing. Tom Golden has written a valuable resource about the grief process of men in our culture.

Goldman, Linda. (1991). *Helping the Grieving Child in School: Opportunities to Help and Enhance Learning*. Bloomington, IN: Phi Beta Kappa International. A practical guide to help the grieving children in the school system.

Goldman, Linda. (1996). *Breaking the Silence: A Guide to Help Children with Complicated Grief Suicide, Homicide, AIDS, Violence, and Abuse*. Philadelphia, PA: Taylor and Francis. A resource guide for parents and professionals to work with children with these complicated grief issues.

Harpham, Wendy. (1997). *When a Parent Has Cancer*. New York, NY: Harper-Collins. A guide to caring for children when a parent has cancer.

Heavilin, Marilyn. (1987). *Roses in December*. San Bernadino, CA: Here's Life. The author expresses a deep understanding of the grieving process, having experienced the death of three children.

Holland, John. (1997). *Coping with Bereavement: A Handbook for Teachers*. Cardiff, Great Britain: Cardiff Academic Press. A clearly written book to help teachers and other educators gain insights into the grieving child in the schools.

Huntley, Theresa. (1991). *Helping Children Grieve when Someone They Love Dies*. Minneapolis, MN: Augsburg Fortress. An easy to read resource for caring adults that honestly addresses children's grief.

Ilse, Sherokee. (1982). *Empty Arms*. Maple Plain, MN: Wintergren. This is a practical book for anyone who has experienced infant death or miscarriage. It offers suggestions and support for decision making at the time of loss and future concerns and grief work.

Jones, Robin. (1995). *Where Was God at 9:02 a.m.?* Nashville, TN: Thomas Nelson. A realistic account of the Oklahoma bombing, and the death, loss, trauma, and healing that followed.

Kubler-Ross, Elisabeth. (1975). *On Death and Dying*. Englewood, NJ: Prentice-Hall. A pioneering book on the subject of death and dying, using real life situations to create true understanding.

Kubler-Ross, Elisabeth. (1985). *On Children and Dying*. New York, NY: Macmillan. Elisabeth Kubler-Ross offers the families of dead and dying children honest information, helpful ideas, and strength to cope.

Kushner, Harold. (1981). *When Bad Things Happen to Good People*. New York, NY: Avon. Following his son's illness and subsequent death, Rabbi Kushner shares his thoughts and feelings of why we suffer.

Leon, Irving. (1990). *When a Baby Dies*. New Haven, CT: Yale University. The first book to explore therapeutically the loss of a baby during pregancy or as a newborn.

Levine, Stephen. (1987). *Healing into Life and Death*. New York, NY: Anchor Press. Stephen Levine explores ways to open our hearts to healing.

Linn, Erin. (1990). *150 Facts About Grieving Children*. Incline Village, NV: The Publisher's Mark. A series of 150 paragraphs discussing important information and understandings about the grieving child.

McCue, Kathleen. (1994). *How to Help Children Through a Parent's Serious Illness*. New York, NY: St. Martin's. Supportive and practical advice on how to help children through a parent's serious illness.

Miller, Alice. (1984). *For Your Own Good*. New York, NY: Farrar, Straus, and Giroux. Alice Miller explores the repercussions of adults taking over a child's will.

Monahon, Cynthia. (1993). *Children and Trauma*. New York, NY: Lexington Books. A guide for parents on helping children heal after trauma.

Moustakas, Clark. (1992). *Psychotherapy with Children*. Greeley, CO: Carron. A classic text in understanding the therapeutic environment.

O'Toole, Donna and Cory Jerre. (1988). *Helping Children Grieve and Grow*. Burnsville, NC: Compassion Books. A wonderful guide for any caring adult working with the grieving child.

Quackenbush, Jamie and Denise Graveline. (1985). *When Your Pet Dies*. New York, NY: Pocket Books. A book for pet owners to help understand feelings when a pet dies.

Rando, Theresa. (1988). *How to Go on Living When Someone You Love Dies*. New York, NY: Lexington Books. A helpful and informative book addressing grief and how to work with it.

Rosenthal, Howard. (1998). *Favorite Counseling and Therapy Techniques*. Philadelphia, PA. Taylor and Francis. This book gathers favorite therapy techniques from 51 well known therapists.

Sanders, Catherine. (1992). *How to Survive the Loss of a Child*. Rocklin, CA: Prima. Provides information on filling the emptiness and rebuilding your life after the loss of a child.

Schneider, John. (1994). *Finding My Way*. Colfax: WI: Seasons Press. A journey of healing and transformation through loss and grief.

Shamoo, Tonia and Philip Patros. (1990). *I Want to Kill Myself*. Lexington, MA: Lexington Books. A guide to helping children cope with depression and suicidal thoughts.

Silverman, Phyliss. (1999). *Never Too Young to Know: Death in Children's Lives*. Oxford University Press. An excellent multifaceted approach on how children experience death includes supporting research data.

Smilansky, Sara. (1987). *On Death (Helping Children Understand and Cope)*. New York, NY: Peter Lang. The author bases her studies on children and their grief process in Tel Aviv.

Trout, Susan. (1990). *To See Differently*. Washington, DC: Three Roses Press. This is an excellent book to help readers heal after experiencing many life issues. A chapter on working with feelings about death is included.

Trout, Susan. (1996). *Born to Serve*. Alexandria, VA: Three Roses Press. This is a unique book that deals deeply and affectively with levels of service.

" A person is a person,
no matter how small. "

By Dr. Seuss

Webb, Nancy Boyd. (1993). *Helping Bereaved Children*. New York, NY: Guilford Press. A handbook for practitioners on helping the bereaved child.

Wolfelt, Alan. (1992). *Sarah's Journey*. Fort Collins, CO: Center for Loss and Life Transition. Eight-year-old Sarah's father suddenly died. Dr. Wolfelt presents three years of Sarah's grief experience and provides counseling perspectives and guidelines for caring adults.

Worden, J. William. (1991). *Grief Counseling and Grief Therapy*. New York, NY: Springer. A comprehensive handbook for grief counseling.

Zinner, Ellen and Mary Beth Williams (Ed.). (1999). *When a Community Weeps*. Philadelphia, PA: Taylor and Francis. This is a community effort of professionals to assist communities with group survivorship.

VIDEOS FOR CHILDREN

O'Toole, Donna. (1994). *Aarvy Aardvark Finds Hope*. Burnesville, NC: Compassion Books. The grief journey of Aarvy is presented through puppets and music for young children.

Rogers, Fred. (1993). *Mr. Rogers Talks About Living and Dying*. Pittsburgh, PA: Family Com. A video for young children on death.

VIDEOS FOR ADULTS

A Child's View of Grief. Alan Wolfelt. (1991). Fort Collins, CO: Center for Loss and Life Transition. A 20-minute video with real children and parents sharing stories and emotions.

Dougy's Place: A 20-20 Video. (1992). Portland, OR: The Dougy Center. A candid look at kids participating in the Dougy Center's Program.

To Touch a Grieving Heart. (1994). Salt Lake City, UT: Panacom Video. This film shows a heartfelt approach to family grief.

What About Me? Kids & Grief. Northbrook, IL: Film Ideas. A great video made totally by using children and their experiences with grief.

What Do I Tell My Children? (1992). Leslie Kussman. Wellesley: MA: Aquarian Productions. A film narrated by Joanne Woodward showing experts, adults, and children exploring feelings regarding death.

When Grief Comes To School. (1991). Carol and David Ebeling. Bloomington, IN: Blooming Educational Enterprises. A film and manual showing families and school personnel discussing grief issues.

When a Parent Dies: Supporting the Children. (1998). This Is a Community in Crisis Teleconference by SCI and Loma Linda University Medical Center, featuring Martin Luther King III, and a national panel of experts on children and grief. SCI-PR#-800-9CARING. (no charge)

CURRICULA AND MANUALS

Bitney, James and Beverly Title. (1996). *The No-Bullying Program*. Minneapolis, MN: Johnson Institute. This is a curriculum developed for specific grades to prevent bully/victim violence in the school.

Boggeman, Sally, Hoerr, Tom and Chrisine Wallach (Ed.). (1996). *Succeeding with Multiple Intelligences*. St. Louis, MO: The New City School. A manual for educators teaching through the personal intelligences.

Celotta, Beverly. (1991). *Generic Crisis Intervention Procedures*. Gaithersburg, MD: Beverly Celotta. A useful school guide for youth suicide.

Cunningham, Linda. (1990). *Teen Age Grief* (TAG). Panarama City, CA: Teen Age Grief. An excellent manual for teen griefwork.

Fitzgerald, Helen. (1998). *Grief at School*. Washington, DC: American Hospice Foundation. A usable grief manual for school personnel.

Klicker, Ralph. (1990). *A Student Dies, a School Mourns. Are You Prepared?* Buffalo, NY: Thanos Institute. A guide to reduce effects of personal loss and suffering in a school community when death occurs.

Lagorio, Jeanne. (1991). *Life Cycle Education Manual*. Solana Beach, CA: Empowerment in Action. A teacher's guide to help with loss issues, including specific lesson plans and guided book activities.

Perschey, Mary. (1997). *Helping Teens Work Through Grief*. Philadelphia, PA: Taylor & Francis. A manual that explains teen grief and then provides useful activities and resources to use with teens.

O'Toole, Donna. (1989). *Growing Through Grief*. Burnsville, NC: Mt. Compassion. A great K–12 curriculum to help children through loss.

Ward, Barbara. (1993). *Good Grief*. London, England: Jessica Kingsley. This manual gives specific classroom lessons for children under eleven.

BOOK SERVICES

Centering Corporation. Omaha, NE. Marv and Joy Johnson have created a comprehensive grief resource center offering publications and trainings on topics of loss and grief. 402-553-1200.

Compassion Book Service. Burnesville, NC. Donna O'Toole provides a wealth of resources and training tools that include books, videos, and cassettes dealing with loss, death, dying, and hope. 704-675-9687.

Mental Health Resources. Saugerties, NY. A complete grief resource for children and families. 914-247-0116.

Self-Esteem Shop. Resource Center. Royal Oak, MI. A "one-stop" resource center to meet the needs of teachers and mental health professionals. 800-251-8336.

Western Psychological Services (WPS). Los Angeles, CA. 800-648-8857. An excellent service for therapists and counselors providing therapeutic tools.

WEBSITES: CHILDREN AND GRIEF

ADEC American Death Education and Counseling Association   www.adec.org

Children of Separation and Divorce Center   http://aspen.newc.com/cosd

Compassionate Friends   www.compassionatefriends.org

Crisis, Grief, and Healing   www.webhealing.com

Death Education Resource   www.death.ed.com

D'Esopo Pratt Resource Center   www.safeplacetogrieve.com

Dougy Center for Grieving Children   www.dougy.org

Helping Children Dealing With Grief   www.erols.com/lgold

CD-ROMs

Team Up to Save Lives: What Every School Should Know About Suicide. (1996). Institute for Juvenile Resources. A CD for schools on suicide. 800-627-7646.

Helping the Grieving Child in School by Linda Goldman. (1999). Kidspeace. A CD-ROM training for educators and professionals on the grieving child. 610-799-8338.

BOOKS FOR CHILDREN

Books About Death

Bode, Janet. (1993). *Death Is Hard to Live with*. New York, NY: Dell. Teens discuss the different ways they cope with death. For teens.

Brown, Margaret Wise. (1979). *The Dead Bird*. New York, NY: Dell. A story of four children who find a dead bird, bury it, and hold a funeral service. Ages 4–8.

Campbell, Dr. James A. (1992). *The Secret Places*. Omaha, NE: Centering Corporation. The story of Ryan and his journey through grief allows children and adults to gain an in-depth look at childhood grief. Ages 6–12.

Dodge, Nancy. (1984). *Thumpy's Story: The Story of Grief and Loss Shared by Thumpy the Bunny*. Springfield, IL: Prairie Lark Press. The story of the death of Thumpy's sister, who was not strong enough to keep living. Ages 5–12.

Ferguson, Dorothy. (1992). *A Bunch of Balloons*. Omaha, NE: Centering Corporation. A resource to help grieving children understand their loss and how it feels after someone dies. Ages 5–8.

Kolf, June Cerza. (1990). *Teenagers Talk About Grief*. Grand Rapids, MI: Baker Book House. A book written especially for and about teenage grief with an account of many first-hand experiences. For teenagers.

Oehler, Jerri. (1978). *The Frog Family's Baby Dies*. Durham, NC: Duke University Medical Center. A coloring story book for very young children discussing sibling loss. Ages 3–6.

O'Toole, Donna. (1988). *Aarvy Ardvark Finds Hope*. (Adult manual available). Burnsville, NC: Compassion Books. Stories of animals that present the pain, sadness, and eventual hope after death. Ages 5–8.

Scravani, Mark. *Love, Mark*. Syracuse, NY: Hope For Bereaved. Letters written to grieving children to help them express their feelings. Ages 7–12.

Varley, Susan. (1984). *Badger's Parting Gifts*. New York, NY: Morrow and Co. Badger was a special friend to all the animals. After his death, each friend recalls a special memory of him. All ages.

White, E. B. (1952). *Charlotte's Web*. New York, NY: Harper and Row. Through the eyes of the farm animals, life and death are sweetly portrayed. Ages 8–13.

Books About Death of a Pet

Biale, Rachel. (1995). *My Pet Died*. Berkely, CA: Tricycle Press. A special memory book for young children who have experienced the death of a pet. Ages 4–8.

Carrick, Carol. (1976). *The Accident*. New York, NY: Clarion Books. Christopher's dog is killed by a truck. He deals with his feelings as he prepares to bury his dog.

Cohen, Miriam. (1984). *Jim's Dog Muffin*. New York, NY: Dell. Jim's dog, Muffin, is killed, and everyone in his first grade class is sad and tries to help him feel better. Ages 5–8

Montgomery, H. and M. Montgomery. (1991). *Good-Bye My Friend*. Minneapolis, MN: Montgomery Press. A series of vignettes honoring the grief involved with the death of a pet. Suggestions on commemorating and remembering animals are included. Ages 8–13.

Rogers, Fred. (1988). *When a Pet Dies*. New York, NY: G. P. Putnam Sons. A first experience book using photographs and words to show what we can do and feel when a pet dies. Ages 4–7.

Sanford, Doris. (1986). *It Must Hurt a Lot*. Portland, OR: Multnomah Press. A boy learns to express his emotions and hold fond his memories after his dog is killed. Ages 4–10

Stein, Sarah. (1974). *About Dying*. New York, NY: Walker and Co. Simple text and photographs to help young children understand death, including a discussion about children's feelings for adults. Ages 3–6.

Viorst, Judith. (1971). *The Tenth Good Thing About Barney*. New York, NY: Atheneum. The story of a pet cat that dies and how we can use funerals and other ways of commemorating with children. Ages 4–8.

Books About Death of a Parent

Blume, Judy. (1981). *Tiger Eyes*. New York, NY: Macmillan Children's Group. Fifteen-year-old Davey works through the feelings of his father's murder in a store hold up. Ages 11 and up.

Douglas, Eileen. (1990). *Rachel and the Upside Down Heart*. Los Angeles, CA: Price Stern Sloan. The true story of four-year-old Rachel, and how her father's death affects her life. Ages 5–9

Frost, Dorothy. (1991). *DAD! Why'd You Leave Me?* Scottdale, PA: Herald Press. This is a story about ten-year-old Ronnie who can't understand why his dad died. Ages 8–12.

Greenfield, Eloise. (1993). *Nathaniel Talking*. New York, NY: Black Butterfly Children's Group.

Nathaniel, an energetic nine-year-old, help us understand a black child's world after his mom dies. He uses rap and rhyme to express his feelings. Ages 7–11.

Klein, Lee. (1995). *The Best Gift for Mom*. Mahwah, NJ: Paulist Press. A story for young children about a boy and his feelings for his dad who had died when he was a baby. Ages 7–12.

Krementz, Jill. (1996). *How It Feels When a Parent Dies*. New York, NY: Knoph. Eighteen children (ages 7–16) speak openly words about their feelings and experiences after the death of a parent.

Lanton, Sandy. (1991). *Daddy's Chair*. Rockville, MD: Kar-Ben Copies. Michael's dad died. The book follows the Shiva, the Jewish week of mourning. He doesn't want anyone to sit in Daddy's chair. Ages 5–10.

LeShan, Eda. (1975). *Learning to Say Goodbye When a Parent Dies*. New York, NY: Macmillan Publishing Co. Written directly to children about problems to be recognized and overcome when a parent dies. Ages 8–up.

Powell, E. Sandy. (1990). *Geranium Morning*. Minneapolis, MN: Carol Rhoda Books, Inc. A boy's dad is killed in a car accident and a girl's mom is dying. The children share their feelings within a special friendship. Ages 6 and up.

Scrivani, Mark. *I Heard Your Daddy Died*. Omaha, NE: Centering Corporation. A book for young children that describes the special feelings they might have when a dad dies. Ages 6–10.

Tiffault, Benette. (1992). *A Quilt for Elizabeth*. Omaha, NE: Centering Corporation. Elizabeth's grandmother helps her understand her feelings after her father dies. This is a good story to initiate an open dialogue with children. Ages 7 and up.

Thaut, Pamela. (1991). *Spike and Ben*. Deerfield Beach: FL: Health Com. The story of a boy whose friend's mom dies. Ages 5–8.

Vigna, Judith. (1991). *Saying Goodbye to Daddy*. Niles, IL: Albert Whitman. A sensitive story about a dad's death and the healing that takes place in the weeks that follow. Ages 5–8.

Books About Sibling Death

Alexander, Sue. (1983). *Nadia the Willful*. New York, NY: Pantheon. Nadia's older brother dies, and she helps her father heal his grief by willfully talking about her brother. Ages 6–10.

Erling, Jake and Susan Erling. (1986). *Our Baby Died. Why?* Maple Plain, MN: Pregnancy and Infant Loss Center. A little boy shares his thoughts and feelings about the birth of his stillborn brother and eventual birth of sibling twins. Children can read, draw, and color this book. Ages 4–10.

Linn, Erin. (1982). *Children Are Not Paperdolls*. Springfield, IL: Human Services Press. Kids who have had brothers and sisters die draw and comment on their experiences. Ages 8–12.

Gryte, Marilyn. (1991). *No New Baby*. Omaha, NE: Centering Corporation. Siblings express feelings about mom's miscarriage. Ages 5–8.

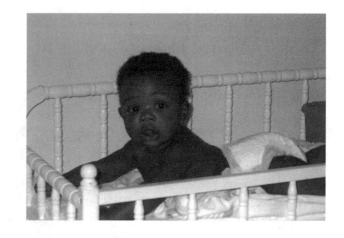

Johnson, Joy and Marv Johnson. (1982). *Where's Jess?* Omaha, NE: Centering Corporation. A book for young children that addresses the questions and feelings kids have when a sibling dies. Ages 4–7.

Richter, Elizabeth. (1986). *Losing Someone You Love: When a Brother or Sister Dies*. New York, NY: Putnam. Adolescents share feelings and experiences about the death of a sibling. Ages 11 and up.

Romond, Janis. (1989). *Children Facing Grief*. St. Meinrad, IN: Abbey Press. Letters from bereaved brothers and sisters, telling of their experiences and offering hope. Ages 6–14.

Sims, Alicia. (1986). *Am I Still a Sister?* Slidell, LA: Big A and Co. This story was written by an eleven-year-old who experienced her baby brother's death. Ages 8–12.

Temes, Roberta. (1992). *The Empty Place*. Far Hills, NJ: Small Horizons. The story of a third grade boy whose older sister dies. Ages 5–9.

Books About a Friend's Death

Blackburn, Lynn. (1987). *Timothy Duck*. Omaha, NE: Centering Corporation. Timothy Duck's friend, John, gets sick and dies. Timothy shares his feelings with others. Ages 5–8.

Blackburn, Lynn. (1991). *The Class in Room 44*. Omaha, NE: Centering Corporation. The children in Room 44 share their feelings of grief when their classmate, Tony, dies. Ages 6–10.

Cohen, Janice. (1987). *I Had a Friend Named Peter*. New York, NY: William Morrow. Betsy's friend, Peter, dies suddenly. She learns through parents and teachers that Peter's memory can live on. Ages 5–10.

Gootman, Marilyn. (1994) *When a Friend Dies*. Minneapolis, MN: Free Spirit Press. This is a book for teens about grieving and healing when a friend dies. For teens

Kaldhol, M. and O. Wenche. (1987). *Goodbye Rune*. New York, NY: Kane-Miller. A story about the drowning death of a girl's best friend and how parents can help. 5–12 years

Kubler-Ross, Elisabeth. (1987). *Remember the Secret*. Berkeley, CA: Celestial Arts. The imaginative story of love and faith of two children, and their experience with death. Ages 5–10.

Park, Barbara. (1995). *Mick Harte Was Here*. New York, NY: Random House. A chapter book about a boy that dies and how it affects the life of the kids that knew him. Ages 8–13.

Books About Grandparent Death

Holden, L. Dwight. (1989). *Gran-Gran's Best Trick*. New York, NY: Magination Press. This book deals directly with cancer. It follows the treatment, sickness, and death of a grandparent. Ages 6–12.

Limb, Sue. (1993). *Come Back, Grandma*. New York, NY: Alfred A. Knopf. A lovely story about a little girl's love for her Grandma through death. Ages preschool to 7.

Liss-Levinson, Nechama. (1995). *When a Grandparent Dies*. Woodstock, VT: Jewish Lights Publishing. A kid's own remembering workbook for dealing with Shiva and the year beyond. Ages 8–13.

Pomerantz, Barbara. (1983). *Bubby, Me, and Memories*. New York, NY: Union Of American Hebrew Congregations. A child's grandmother dies. His feelings are addressed and his questions answered. Good source to explain Jewish rituals. Ages 5–8.

Thomas, Jane. (1988). *Saying Goodbye to Grandma*. New York, NY: Clarion. A sensitively written book about a family joining together for grandma's funeral. Ages 4–8.

Thornton, Terence. (1987). *Grandpa's Chair*. Portland, OR: Multnomah Press. The story of a small boy's love for his grandfather, his last visit to see him, and his grandfather's eventual death. Ages 4–8.

Books About Hospice

Carney, Karen and William Pilkington. (1995). *Everything Changes, but Love Endures*. Wethersfield, CT: D'Esopo–Pratt Resource Center. This is a wonderful storybook for young children that clearly explains hospice to them. Ages 5–10.

Flynn, Jessie. (1994). *What Is Hospice?* Louisville, KY: A book for young children explaining hospice. Ages 3–7.

Books About Death Through War

Bunting, Eve. (1990). *The Wall*. New York, NY: Clarion Books. Illustrations and story about a father and son that visit the Vietnam Veterans Memorial and the impact of war on their lifes. Ages 5–8.

Coerr, Eleanor. (1993). *Sadako and the Thousand Paper Cranes*. New York, NY: Putnam. This is a true story about a Japanese girl who is dying from her exposure to radiation from the bomb at Hiroshima. Her hope for peace and life is symbolized in her paper cranes. Ages 8–13.

McDaniel, Lurlene. (1992). *When Happily Ever After Ends*. New York, NY: Bantam Books. A story about a teenage girl whose dad killed himself after the Vietnam War. Ages 10 and up.

Workbooks on Death for Children

Boulden, Jim and Joan Boulden. (1991). *Saying Goodbye*. Santa Rosa, CA: Boulden. A bereavement workbook and coloring book for young children. Ages 5–8.

Goldman, Linda. (1998). *Bart Speaks Out on Suicide*. Los Angeles, CA: WPS. This is an interactive workbook for young children who have had someone die from suicide.

Haasl, Beth and Jean Marnocha. (1990). *Bereavement Support Group Program for Children*. Muncie, IN: Accelerated Development, Inc. A step-by-step workbook for children (with leader manual) to use in a bereavement group. Ages 8–13.

Hammond, Janice. (1980) *When My Mommy Died* and *When My Daddy Died*. Flint, MI: Cranbrook Publishing. Both workbooks are geared to young children's bereavement work and parent death.

Heegaard, Marge. (1988). *When Someone Very Special Dies*. Minneapolis, MN: Woodland Press.

An excellent workbook that uses art work and journeling to allow children to work through their grief. A facilitator's manual is available. Ages 5-12.

O'Toole, Donna. (1995). *Facing Change*. Burnsville, NC: Compassion Books. An excellent guide and workbook for pre-teens and teens. Ages 11 and up.

Rogers, Fred. (1991). *So Much to Think About*. Pittsburgh, PA: Family Communications. An activity book for young children when someone they love has died. Ages 5-8.

Traisman, Enid Samuel. (1992). *Fire in My Heart: Ice in My Veins*. Omaha, NE: Centering Corporation. A wonderful workbook for teenagers to explore thoughts and feelings and record grief memories. For teenagers.

Memory Book

Chimeric, Inc. (1991). *Illustory*. Denver, CO. Kids can write and illustrate their own books, which are then sent away and made into a hardcover bound book with the original text. Ages 5–10.

Books about Life Cycles

Brown, Laura and Marc Brown. (1996). *When Dinosaurs Die*. New York, NY: Little, Brown & Co. This is a wonderful and practical guide for children in helping them understand and deal with real concerns and feelings about death. Ages 5-11.

Buscaglia, Leo. (1982). *The Fall of Freddie the Leaf*. Thorofare, NJ: Charles B. Slack. The story of the changing seasons as a metaphor for life and death. Ages 4-8.

Gerstein, Mordica. (1987). *The Mountains of Tibet*. New York, NY: Harper and Row. The story of a woodcutter's journey from the mountains of Tibet through the universe of endless choices and back to his home again. Ages 7 and up.

Goble, Paul. (1993). *Beyond the Ridge*. New York, NY: Aladdin Books. This book captues the essence of the Native American belief system on dying and death and the great circle of life. Ages 5-10.

Hoban, Tana. (1971). *Look Again*. New York, NY: Macmillan. A book of photographs that illustrate to children that we can't always know the larger picture when we see only one small part. Ages 4-7.

Mellonie, Bryan and Robert Ingpen. (1983). *Lifetimes: The Beautiful Way to Explain Death to Children*. New York, NY: Bantam Books. Explains the ongoing life cycle of plants, animals, and people. Ages 3–10.

Munsch, Robert. (1983). *Love You Forever*. Willowdale, Canada: A Firefly Book. A beautiful book for adults and children alike about the continuance of love throughout life. All ages.

Wood, Douglas. (1992). *Old Turtle*. Duluth, MN: Pfeifer-Hamilton. A fable for children and adults that captures the message of peace on earth and oneness with nature. The illustrations are beautiful. Ages 5 and up.

Books About Aging Grandparents

De Paola, Tommy. (1980). *Now One Foot Now the Other*. New York, NY: G. P. Putnam Sons. The story of a grandfather's stroke and how it affects his grandchildren. Ages 5–8.

Farber, Norma. (1979). *How Does It Feel to Be Old?* New York, NY: E. P. Dutton. A grandmother talks about how she feels to be old. A good book for grandparents and grandchildren to share. Ages 6–12.

Miles, Miska. (1971). *Annie and the Old One*. Boston, MA: Joy St. Books. A Navaho girl's aging grandmother gets ready to die. She attempts to undo the weaving of a rug to stop this dying process. Ages 6–12.

Books About Alzheimer's

Nelson, Vacinda. (1988). *Always Grandma*. New York, NY: South China Printing. A grandmother develops Alzheimer's disease and her grandchild learns to live with her present condition and hold memories of her when she was healthy. Ages 5–8.

Books About Adult Illness

Fine, Judylaine. (1986). *Afraid to Ask*. New York, NY: Beech Tree Books. This book is written for teens and their families to share about cancer. Teens and up.

Goodman, Michael B. (1991). *Vanishing Cookies*. Mississauga, Canada: Arthur Jones Lithographing. A book that talks honestly about a parent's cancer treatment. Ages 6–13.

Hazouri, Sandra and Miriam McLaughlin. (1994). *My Family Is Living with Cancer* (Workbook and Storybook). Warminster, PA: Mar-co. A story and accompanying activity book for helping children who have a family member with cancer. Ages 6–10.

Heegaard, Marge. (1991). *When Someone Has a Very Special Illness*. Minneapolis, MN: Woodland Press. Practical workbook that addresses feelings when a parent is sick. Children can illustrate it themselves. Ages 6–12.

Kohlenberg, Sherry. (1994). *Sammy's Mommy Has Cancer*. New York, NY: Magination Press. This is a book written by a real mom and her son who lived with cancer. Ages 4–8.

LeShan, Eda. (1986). *When a Parent Is Very Sick*. Boston, MA: Joy Street Books. A helpful book for children and parents that talks openly about the stress of having a parent with a serious illness. Ages 8–13.

Nystrom, Caroline. (1990). *Emma Says Goodbye*. Batavia, IL: Lion Publisher. Emma's aunt has a terminal illness, and Emma comes to visit with her. Ages 8–14.

Parkinson, Carolyn. (1991). *My Mommy Has Cancer*. Rochester, NY: Park Press. This book helps young children learn about cancer, its treatment, and its emotional impact. Ages 4–8.

Strauss, Linda. (1988). *Coping When a Parent Has Cancer*. New York, NY: Rosen. A book for teenagers who are coping with a parent with cancer. For teenagers.

Books about Children's Illness

Baznik, Donna. (1981). *Becky's Story*. Bethesda, MD: ACCH. Becky, a six-year-old, feels confused and left out when her brother is in a bad accident and she feels he is given all the attention. Ages 4–7.

Carney, Karen. (1995). *Barlay and Eve: What is Cancer Anyway?* Wetherfield, CN: D'Esopo Resource Center. A simple and clear explanation of cancer for young children. Ages 4–8.

Dorfman, Elena. (1994). *The C-Word*. Portland, OR: New Sage Press. This is a wonderful book about teenagers and their family living with cancer. Ages 12 and up.

Foss, Karen. (1996). *The Problem with Hair*. Omaha, NE: Centering Corporation. This is a story about a little girl who has cancer and has lost her hair through chemotherapy. Ages 5–10.

Gaes, Jason. (1989). *My Book for Kids with Cansur*. Pierre, SD: Melius-Peterson. The story of eight-year-old Jason who successfully battles cancer. Jason's brothers illustrate the book. Ages 7–12.

Lawrence, Melinda. (1987). *My Life: Melinda's Story*. Alexandria, VA: Children's Hospice International. A story by Melinda and her journey through illness. Ages 5 and up.

Maple, Marilyn. (1992). *On the Wings of a Butterfly*. Seattle, WA: Parenting Press. A butterfly becomes a friend to Lisa, a child dying of cancer. Lisa shares her fears of dying. Ages 5–10.

Sanford, Doris. (1992). *No Longer Afraid*. Sisters, OR: Multnomah Press. This is a story about a child living with cancer that gets to participate in the Make A Wish program.

Schultz, Charles M. (1990). *Why, Charlie Brown, Why?* New York, NY: Topper Books. The story about Charlie's friend Janice, who has leukemia, and what happens when a friend is very ill. Ages 5–10.

Stolp, Hans. (1990). *The Golden Bird*. New York, NY: Dial Books. An eleven-year-old boy is terminally ill and explores his thoughts and feelings about death.

Tartakoff, Katy. (1994). *My Stupid Illness*. Denver, CO: The Children's Legacy. This is an interactive book for children undergoing cancer treatment that helps them to write their thoughts and feelings. Ages 5–10.

Books About Organ Donor and Tissue Transplant

Carney, Karen. (1999). *Precious Gifts: Katie Coolican's Story: Barlay and Eve Explain Organ and Tissue Donation*. A sensitive resource explaining these delicate issues to young children. Ages 4–8.

Flynn, Jesse. (1996). *A New Heart For Hannah*. Louisville, KY: Accord. A book written for very young children about organ donors. Ages 4–7.

Books About Down's Syndrome

Cairo, Shelley, Jasmine Cairo, and Tara Cairo. (1985). *Our Brother Has Down's Snydrome*. Ontario, Canada: Annick Press LTD. A loving book that explains Down's Syndrome to young children through facts and photographs. Ages 5–8.

O'Shaughnessy, Ellen. (1992). *Somebody Called Me a Retard Today . . . and My Heart Felt Sad*. New York, NY: Walker and Co. A lovely book explains in a very simple way how a young mentally challenged girl feels when she is confronted with being different. Ages 5–adult.

Books About AIDS

Fassler, David. (1990). *What's a Virus, Anyway?* Burlington, VT: Waterfront Press. This is a well done children's book explaining concepts about the AIDS virus. Ages 5–9.

Hausherr, Rosemare. (1989). *Children and the AIDS Virus*. New York, NY: Clarion Books. An informative book for older and younger children that tells and shows through pictures the world of AIDS. Ages 5 and up.

Jordan, MaryKate. (1989). *Losing Uncle Tim*. Niles, IL: A. Whitman Niles. Daniel's Uncle Tim dies of AIDS, and Daniel struggles with many feelings about it. Ages 6–10.

Kittredge, Mary. (1991). *Teens with AIDS Speak Out*. New York, NY: Simon & Schuster. An excellent resource for teens who speak out about their own journey with AIDS. For teenagers.

McCauslin, Mark. (1995). *Update: AIDS*. Parsippany, NJ: Crestwood House. An excellent resource for middle school children on the topic of AIDS. Ages 9–13.

McDaniel, Lurlene. (1993). *Baby Alicia Is Dying*. New York, NY: Bantam Books. A book for teens about a baby that was infected with the HIV virus. Ages 11 and up.

Merrifield, Margaret. (1990). *Come Sit by Me*. Ontario, Canada: Women's Press. A great book for parents and teachers to educate young children on the facts about AIDS. Ages 4–8.

Moutoussamy-Ashe, Jeanne. (1993). *Daddy and Me*. New York: NY: Alfred Knoph. A wonderful photo story of Arthur Ashe and his daughter, Camera, sharing life with his illness. Ages 4 and up.

Sanford, Doris. (1991). *David Has AIDS*. Portland, OR: Multnomah Press. David struggles with the disease of AIDS. Ages 7–11.

Verniero, Joan. (1995). *You Can Call Me Willy*. New York, NY: Magination Press. This is a story for children about AIDS. Ages 5–10.

Wolf, Bernard. (1997). *HIV Positive*. New York, NY: Dutton Children's Books. An excellent resource for children includes photographs and honest explanations about HIV and AIDS. Ages 8–13.

Books About Asthma

Rogers, Allison. (1987). *Luke Has Asthma*. Burlington, VT: Waterfront Books. The story of Luke and his life with asthma. Ages 3–7.

Books About Weight Disorders and Eating Problems

Berry, Joy. (1990). *About Weight Problems and Eating Disorders*. Chicago, IL: Children's Press. An interesting book that explains the realities of eating disorders and weight problems. Ages 7–13.

Books About Childhood Diabetes

Betschart, Jean. (1991). *A Workbook on Diabetes for Children*. Minneapolis, MN: DCI Publishing. This is an easy to understand workbook for children to help them manage diabetes. Ages 6–12.

Mulder, Linnea. (1992). *Sarah and Puffle*. New York, NY: Magination Press. A book to help children and their family cope with diabetes. Ages 5–9.

Books About Children that Stop Growing

Russo, Marisabina. (1990). *Alex Is My Friend*. New York, NY: Greenwillow Books. The story of a boy whose good friend is a dwarf. He realizes that although his friend does not grow, their friendship deepens through time and they continue to have fun together. Ages 5–8.

Books About Stranger Anxiety and/or Elective Mutism

Schaefer, Charles. (1992). *Cat's Got Your Tongue*. New York, NY: Magination Press. This is a story of Anna, a kindergartener diagnosed as an electively mute child. Children with stranger anxieties also can relate to Anna's behaviors. Ages 3–7.

Books About Moving

Blume, Judy. (1986). *Are You There God? It's Me Margaret*. New York, NY: Dell Publishing. Margaret has to face moving and beginning a new life. Especially good for girls in grades 3 through 7.

Johnson, Angela. (1992). *The Leaving Morning*. New York, NY: Orchard Books. A book about the feelings a family goes through during a move, and everything and everyone they need to say good-bye to. Ages 5–8.

McKend, Heather. (1988). *Moving Gives Me a Stomachache*. Ontario, Canada: Black Moss Press. The story of a child's anxiety and fear of moving. Ages 5–8.

Books About Divorce

Boulden, J. and J. Boulden (1991). *Let's Talk*. Santa Rosa, CA: Boulden. A kid's activity book for separation and divorce. Ages 5–8.

Evans, Marla D. (1989). *This Is Me and My Single* Parent. New York, NY: Magination Press. A discovery workbook for children and single parents. Ages 8–13.

Fassler, D., M. Lash, and S. Ives. (1988). *Changing Families*. Burlington, VT: Waterfront Books. Advice for parents and children coping with divorce, remarriage, and new families. Ages 4–12.

Heegaard, Marge. (1990). *When Mom and Dad Separate*. Minneapolis, MN: Woodland Press. A workbook for children exploring thoughts and feelings about separation and divorce. Ages 6–12.

Krementz, Jill. (1988). *How It Feels When Parents Divorce*. New York, NY: Knoph. Many different kinds of children describe how the divorce of their parents has affected them. Ages 8–13.

Rogers, Fred. (1996). *Let's Talk About Divorce*. New York, NY: G. P. Putnam. A beautiful book with photographs explaining divorce to young children. Ages 5–8.

Sanford, Doris. (1985). *Please Come Home*. Portland, OR: Multnomah Press. Jenny's thoughts and feelings are expressed to her teddy bear about her parents divorce. Ideas for adults to help children are included. Ages 7–12.

Books About Remarriage

Heegaard, Marge. (1993). *When a Parent Marries Again*. Minneapolis, MN: Woodland Press. An excellent resource for children that speaks to the many complicated feelings involved with a parent remarrying. Ages 5–10.

Rogers, Fred. (1997). *Let's Talk About Stepfamilies*. New York, NY: G. P. Putnam. An excellent discussion for young children on the topic of stepfamilies. Ages 5–10.

Books About Adoption

Banish, R. and Jordan-Wong, J. (1992). *A Forever Family*. New York, NY: Harper Collins. Eight-year-old Jennifer was in many foster homes before being adopted as as a part of her forever family. Ages 5–8.

Girard, Linda. (1989). *We Adopted You Benjamin, Koo*. Niles, IL: A. Whitman and Co. Benjamin is a nine-year-old boy from another country. He tells of how he adjusted to adoption and a culturally blended family.

Hicks, Randall. (1995). *Adoption Stories for Young Children*. Sun City, CA: Wordslinger Press. This book with photos tells an adoption story to young children. Ages 4–8.

Sanford, Doris. (1989). *Brian Was Adopted*. Portland, OR: Multnomah Press. Brian questions many parts of adoption and talks to God about it. Ages 5–11.

Stinson, Kathy. (1992). *Steven's Baseball Mitt*. Ontario, Canada: Annick Press. The thoughts and feelings that go through an adopted child's mind about his birth mother. Ages 5–8.

Books About Homelessness

Kroll, Virginia. (1995). *Shelter Folks*. Grand Rapids, MI: William B. Eerdmans. A sensitive story about a nine-year-old girl who is forced to move into a neighborhood shelter. Ages 6–11.

Nasta, Phyliss. (1991). *Aaron Goes to the Shelter*. Tuscan, AR: Whole Child. A story and workbook guide about abuse, placement, and protective services. Ages 5–12.

Powell, Sandy. (1992). *A Chance to Grow*. Minneapolis, MN: Carolrhoda Books. A book for children about homelessness. Ages 8–11.

Trottier, Maxine. (1997). *A Safe Place*. Morton Grove, IL: Albert Whitman & Co. To escape her dad's abuse, a little girl and her mom find refuge in a shelter. Ages 5–9.

Books About Emotional Abuse

Loftis, Chris. (1995). *The Words Hurt*. Far Hills, NJ: New Horizon Press. A story about a young boy trying to cope with the trauma of verbal abuse.

Books About Sexual Abuse

Girard, Linda. (1984). *My Body Is Private*. Morton Grove, IL: Albert Whitman & Co. This book provides age appropriate ways for children to distinguish between good touching and unwanted touching. Ages 6–11.

Lowery, Linda. (1994). *Laurie Tells*. Minneapolis, MN: Carolhoda Books. A sensitive story about a girl that is sexually abused by her father. Ages 8–13.

Sanford, Doris. (1986). *I Can't Talk About It*. Portland, OR: Multnomah Press. Annie talks to an abstract form, Love, about her sexual abuse, and begins to heal and trust. Ages 8–13.

Sanford, Doris. (1993). *Something Must Be Wrong with Me*. Sisters, OR: Questar. A sensitive story about a young boy's journey with sexual abuse. Ages 5–10.

Books About Suicide

Garland, Sherry. (1994). *I Never Knew Your Name*. New York, NY: Ticknor & Fields. A young boy tells the story of a teenage boy's suicide who name he didn't even know. Ages 5–10.

Goldman, Linda. (1998). *Bart Speaks Out on Suicide*. Los Angeles, CA: WPS Publishers. This is a clear an honest memory book and interactive story book that creates words to use to discuss the topic of suicide with young children. Ages 5–12.

Harper, J. (1993). *Hurting Yourself*. Omaha, NE: Centering Corporation. A resource for young people who have intentionally injured themselves. For teenagers.

Norton, Yuri. (1993). *Dear Uncle Dave*. Hanover, NH: Shirley Baldwin Waring. A story written by a fourth grade girl sharing memories about Uncle Dave and his death by suicide. Ages 5–10.

Kukliln, S. (1994). *After a Suicide: Young People Speak Up*. New York, NY: G. P. Putnam's Sons. This book is a great teen resource with stories by teens who experienced a suicide. For teenagers.

Urich, Jeanette. (1990). *I Wish I Were in a Lonely Meadow: When a Parent Commits Suicide*. Portland, OR: Dougy Center. This is a good resource written by children experiencing a parent's suicide. Ages 9–15.

Books About Depressed Parents

Hamilton, DeWitt. (1995). *Sad Days, Glad Days*. Morton Grove, IL: Albert Whitman & Co. A story about how it feels as a child to have a parent suffering from depression. Ages 6–11.

Rogers, Fred. (1990). *Good Weather or Not*. Homestead, PA: Family Communications, Inc. A good resource for young children about adult depression. Ages 5–9.

Sanford, Doris. (1993). *It Won't Last Forever*. Sisters, OR: Questar Pub. This is a book for children about living with a depressed parent. Ages 6–12.

Books About Abandonment and Foster Care

Lowery, Linda. (1995). *Somebody Somewhere Knows My Name*. Minneapolis, MN: Carolrhoda, Inc. Grace and her brother are abandoned by their mother and stay at a shelter. Ages 8–13.

Sanford, Doris. (1993). *For Your Own Good*. Sisters, OR: Questar. This is a child's book about living in a foster home. Ages 6–11.

Books About Violence

Cohen, Janice. (1994). *Why Did it Happen?* New York, NY: Morrow Junior Books. An excellent resource for children on neighborhood violence. Ages 5–10.

Davis, Diane. (1984). *Something Is Wrong in My House*. Seattle, WA: Parenting Press. A book about parents fighting, ways to cope with violence, and how to break the cycle. Ages 8–12.

Lorbiecki, Marybeth. (1996). *Just One Flick of the Finger*. New York, NY: Dial Books. When a young boy takes a gun to school to scare off a bully, the gun goes off during an argument. Ages 6–11.

Loftis, Chris. (1997). *The Boy Who Sat by the Window*. Far Hills, NJ: New Horizon Press. This is an excellent book for young children about a boy who gets murdered and the cycle of violence surrounding his death. Ages 6–12.

Patterson, Susan. (1990). *I Wish the Hitting Would Stop*. Argo, ND: Red Flag Resources. A workbook and storybook for children living in violent homes. Ages 5–10.

Paris, Susan. (1986). *Mommy and Daddy Are Fighting*. Seattle, WA: Seals Press. Honest discussion of parental fighting with a discussion guide for parents. Ages 5–8.

Winston-Hiller, Randy. (1986). *Some Secrets Are for Sharing*. Denver, CO: MAC Publishing. A story of a family secret of a boy being beaten by his mom. He finally tells and gets help for him and his mom. Ages 6–11.

Wright, Leslie. (1991). *I Love my Dad but...*. Toronto, Ontario: Is Five Press. A book for young children that speaks to the difficult topic of violent family situations. Ages 5–10.

Books About Homicide

Aub, Kathleen. (1995). *Children Are Survivors Too*. Boca Raton. FL: Grief Ed. Enterprises. A child homicide survivors book. Age 6–teens.

Constans, Gabriel. (1997). *Picking up the Pieces*. Warminster, PA: Mar-co produts. A program about violent death. For use with middle school students. Ages 10–13.

Henry-Jenkins, W. (1993). *Just Us*. Omaha, NE: Centering Corporation. This is a book for teens about homicide related deaths. For teens.

Mahon, K. L. (1992). *Just One Tear*. New York, NY: Lothrop, Lee, and Shephard. This is a fictional fourteen-year-old's journal after a homicide and during the trial and outcome. For teenagers.

Smith, I. (1991). *We Don't Like Remembering Them as a Blade of Grass*. Portland, OR: Doughy Center. This is a book by children who have had a loved one murdered. Ages 7–16.

Books About Trauma

Berry, Joy. (1990). *About Traumatic Experiences*. Chicago, IL: Children's Press. Answers to kids' questions about trauma. Ages 8–11.

Salloum, Alison (1998). *Reactions*. Omaha, NE: Centering Corporation. A workbook to help young children who are experiencing trauma and grief. Ages 7–11.

Books About Bullies

Cohen-Posey. (1995). *How to Handle Bullies, Teasers and other Meanies*. Highland City, FL: Rainbow Books. A practical resource for kids to help them with the issues of bullying. Ages 8–13.

Kaufman, Gershen and Lev Raphael. (1990). *Stick up for Yourself*. Minneapolis, MN: Free Spirit Publishing. A guide to help kids feel personal power and self-esteem. Ages 8–12.

Romain, Trevor. (1997). *Bullies Are a Pain in the Brain*. Minneapolis, MN: Free Spirit Publishing. A great book for young children to address the topic of bullies. Ages 7–11.

Books About Natural Disaster

Williams, Vera. (1992). *A Chair for My Mother*. New York, NY: Mulberry Books. After a fire destroys their home, Rosa, her mom, and grandmother save their money for a big chair to share. Ages 5–10.

Books About Families with Alcoholics

Black, Claudia. *My Dad Loves Me, My Dad Has a Disease*. Denver, CO: MAC Publishing. This is a workbook for children of alcoholics to help them better understand alcoholism and their feelings about it. Ages 6–14.

Carbone, Elisa Lynn. (1992). *My Dad's Definitely Not a Drunk*. Burlington, VT: Waterfront Books. A 12-year-old boy struggles with his dad's secret drinking problem, and discovers ways to get help. Ages 9–14.

Hastings, Jill and Marion Typpo. (1984). *An Elephant in the Living Room*. Minneapolis, MN: Comp Care. A workbook about alcoholism that allows children to express their feelings. Ages 8–12.

Sanford, Doris. (1984). *I Know the World's Worst Secret*. Portland, OR: Multnomah Press. A girl talks about her alcoholic mom. Ages 8–13.

Books About Dads

Chaplan, Roberta. (1991). *Tell Me a Story, Paint Me the Sun*. New York, NY: Magination Press. The story of a girl that feels ignored by her father. Ages 8–12.

Cochran, Vicki. (1992). *My Daddy Is a Stranger*. Omaha, NE: Centering Corporation. The story of a little girl whose dad left home when she was a baby and how she feels about his absence. Ages 5–8.

Hickman, Martha. (1990). *When Andy's Father Went to Prison*. Niles: IL: Albert Whitman and Company. Andy's dad was arrested for stealing and put into prison. Andy copes with his feelings of shame and abandonment while his dad's away. Ages 5–9.

Books About Working Parents

Molnar, Dorothy and Stephanie Fenton. (1991). *Who Will Pick Me up When I Fall?* Niles, IL: Albert Whitman and Co. A little girl has difficulty remembering where she goes everyday while both parents are working. Ages 5–8.

Quinlan, Patricia. (1987). *My Dad Takes Care of Me*. Ontario, Canada: Annick Press. The story about a child who has a working mom and a dad who stays home because he doesn't have a job. Ages 5–8.

Books About Immigration

Fassler, David and Kimberly Danworth (1992). *Coming to America: The Kids Book of Immigration*. Burlington, VT: Waterfront Books. Help for children to explore feelings on immigration. Ages 4–12.

Books About Attention Deficit Hyperactivity Disorder

Quinn, Patricia and Stern, Judith (1991). *Putting on the Brakes*. New York, NY: Magination Press. A guide for children to understand and work with ADHD. Ages 8–13.

Books About Dyslexia

Janover, Caroline. (1988). *Josh: A Boy with Dyslexia*. Burlington, VT: Waterfront Books. The story about Josh and his feelings about having dyslexia. Ages 8–12.

Books About Magical Thinking

Blackburn, Lynn. (1991). *I Know I Made It Happen*. Omaha, NE: Centering Corporation. This book presents many circumstances where kids feeling guilty and responsible for making things happen. Ages 5–8.

Flynn, Jessie. (1994). *It's Not Your Fault*. Lexington, KY: Accord. A book for young children that discusses the magical thinking of feeling responsible for the death of a person. Ages 3-7.

Rappaport, Doreen. (1995). *The New King*. New York, NY: Dial Books. A wonderful book about a boy who becomes king after his father dies. He uses magical thinking to try and bring him back to life. Ages 6-12.

Books About Feelings

Crary, Elizabeth. (1992). *I'm Mad* and *I'm Frustrated*. Seattle, WA: Parenting Press. A series of children's books that identify feelings and gives options on what to do with them. Ages 3-8.

Doleski, Teddi. (1983). *The Hurt*. Mahwah, NJ: Paulest Press. The wonderful story about a little boy who keeps all of his hurt inside, until the hurt grows so big it fills his room. When he shares his feelings, the hurt begins to go away. All ages.

Farrington, Liz. (1994). *Nightmares in the Mist*. Palo Alto. CA: Enchante. This is a book that speaks of children's fears and provides ways to use imagination to help overcome them. (Has accompanying workbook.) Ages 6-10.

Hazen, Barbara. (1992). *Even If I Did Something Awful*. New York, NY: Aladdin Books. The reassuring story of a little girl that realizes mom will love her no matter what she does. Ages 5-8.

Jampolsky, G. and D. Cirincione. (1991). *Me First and the Gimme Gimmes*. Deerfield Beach, FL: Health Communication. A story that shows the transformation of selfishness into love. All ages.

Marcus, Irene and Paul Marcus (1990). *Scary Night Visitors*. New York, NY: Magination Press. Davey has fears at night and learns to feel safe through experiencing his feelings directly. Ages 4-7.

Moser, Adolph. (1988). *Don't Pop Your Cork on Monday*. Kansas City, MO: Landmark Editions. A handbook for children to explore the causes of stress and techniques to deal with it Ages 5-8.

Moser, Adolph. (1991). *Don't Feed the Monster on Tuesday*. Kansas City, MO: Landmark Editions. Dr. Moser offers children information on the importance of knowing their own self-worth and ways to improve self-esteem. Ages 5-8.

Oram, Hiawyn. (1982). *Angry Arthur*. New York, NY: E. P. Dutton. Arthur becomes enraged with Mom and creates havoc on the planet. Ages 5-8.

Sanford, Doris, (1986). *Don't Look at Me*. Portland, OR: Multnomah Press. The story of Patrick who feels very stupid and learns to feel special about himself. Ages 7-11.

Simon, Norma. (1989). *I Am Not a Crybaby*. New York, NY: Puffin Books. This book shows how children of different races and cultures share the commonality of feelings. Ages 5–8.

Steig, William. (1988). *Spinky Sulks*. Singapore: Sunburst Books. Spinky is angry and begins to sulk. No one can make him stop. Ages 5–8.

Voirst, Judith. (1972). *Alexander and the Terrible Horrible No Good Very Bad Day*. New York, NY: Aladdin Books. Alexander has a day where everything goes wrong. Everyone can relate to this. Ages 5–8.

Books About New Siblings

Alexander, Martha. (1979). *When the New Baby Comes, I'm Moving Out*. New York, NY: Dial Books. A little boy is angry with his mom for preparing for a new baby. Ages 4–7.

Blume, Judy. (1980). *Superfudge*. New York, NY: Dell Publishing. Peter, a sixth grade boy, learns his mom is having a baby and wonders how he will survive it. A good book for kids in grade three to seven.

Boyd, Lizi. (1990). *Sam Is My Half Brother*. New York, NY: Puffin Books. Hessie is afraid that her new half brother, Sam, will get all the love and attention. This book stimulates discussion on stepfamilies. Ages 4–8.

Books About Cremation

Flynn, Jessie. (1994). *What Is Cremation?* Louisville, KY: Accord. This book provides a very simple explanation of cremation for the young child. Ages 3–7.

Carney, Karen. (1995). *Our Special Garden: Understanding Cremation*. Wethersfield, CT: D'Esopo-Pratt Resource Center. This is a beautifully done book for young children that create words to use on the important topic of cremation. Ages 3-7.

Books About Funerals, Memorial Services, and Rituals

Ancona, G. (1993). *Pablo Remembers*. New York, NY: Lothrop, Lee & Shepard. A book with interesting photographs explaining the Mexican fiesta of the Day Of The Dead. Ages 6–10.

Carson, J. (1992). *You Hold Me and I'll Hold You*. New York, NY: Orchard Books. A story of a little girl's first experience at a memorial service. Ages 5–9.

Balter, Lawrence. (1991). *A Funeral for Whiskers*. Hauppauge, NY: Barron's Educational Series. Sandy's cat dies, and she find useful ways to commemorate. Ages 5–9.

Carney, Karen. (1995). *Barlay and Eve Sitting Shiva*. Wethersfield, CT: D'Esopo-Pratt Resource Center. A good resource for young kids to explain the customs involving the Jewish practice of Shiva. Ages 3–7.

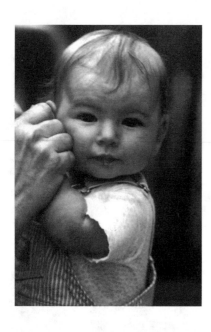

Flynn, Jessie. (1994). *A Visit to the Cemetery*. Louisville, KY: Accord. A simple book for young children explaining a trip to the cemetery. Ages 3–6.

Flynn, Jessie. (1994). *Should I Go to the Funeral?* Louisville, KY: Accord. A simple presentation for young children on reasons to go to a funeral. Ages 3–6.

Techner, D., and J. Hirt-Manheimer. (1993). *A Candle for Grandpa: A Guide to the Jewish Funeral for Children and Parents*. New York, NY: UAHC Press. A children's resource on Jewish funerals and burials. Ages 7–12.

Winsch, Jane. (1995). *After the Funeral*. New York, NY: Paulist Press. A simple book for young children that expresses possible feelings once the funeral is over. Ages 4–7.

Books About Goodbyes

Brillhart, Julie. (1990). *Anna's Goodbye Apron*. Niles, IL: Albert Whitman and Co. A story about how a kindergarten class says goodbye to their wonderful teacher Anna who has to move. Ages 4–7.

Osborne, Judy. (1978). *My Teacher Said GOODBYE Today*. Brookline, MA: Emijo Press. This story shows how the end of the year when kids and teachers need to say goodbye can evoke lots of feelings. Ages 4–6.

Viorst, Judith. (1992). *The Good Bye Book*. New York, NY: Aladdin Books. The story of a child left unwillingly with a babysitter. Ages 4–7.

" *Your children are not your children/They are the sons and daughters of life's longing for itself...*

You are the bows from which your children as living arrows are sent forth. **"**

The Prophet by Kahil Gibran

REFERENCES

Adams, Karen, and Jennifer Fay. (1992). *Helping Your Child Recover from Sexual Abuse*. Seattle, WA: University of Washington Press.

Berry, Joy. (1990). *About Change and Moving*. Chicago, IL: Children's Press.

Berry, Joy. (1990). *About Traumatic Experiences*. Chicago, IL: Children's Press.

Blackburn, Lynn (1991). *I Know I Made It Happen*. Omaha, NE: Centering Corporation.

Bloomfield, Harold and Leonard Felder. (1986). *Achilles Syndrome*. New York: Random House.

Brown, Laura & Marc Brown. (1996). *When Dinosaurs Die*. New York, NY: Little Brown & Co.

Buscaglia, Leo. (1982). *The Fall of Freddie the Leaf*. Thorofare, NJ: Charles B. Slack Co.

Cappacchione, Lucia. (1982). *The Creative Journal for Children*. Boston, MA: Shambhala Publishing, Inc.

Carr, Richard. (1973). *Be a Bird, Be a Frog, Be a Tree*. Garden City, NJ: Doubleday & Co., Inc.

Cohen, Miriam. (1984). *Jim's Dog Muffin*. New York, NY: Dell Publishing.

Davis, Diane. (1984). *Something Is Wrong in My House*. Seattle, WA: Parenting Press, Inc.

De Milleis, Richard. (1973). *Put Your Mother on the Ceiling*. New York, NY: Penguin Books.

Doleski, Teddi. (1983). *The Hurt*. Mahwah, NJ: Paulest Press.

Eberling, Carol and David Eberling. (1991). *When Grief Comes to School*. Bloomington, IN: Bloomington Educational Enterprises.

Fassler, David, Michele Lash, and Sally Ives. (1988). *Changing Families*. Burlington, VT: Waterfront Books.

Ferguson, Dorothy. (1992). *A Bunch of Balloons*. Omaha, NE: Centering Corporation.

Fox, Sandra. (1988). *Good Grief: Helping Groups of Children When a Friend Dies*. Boston, MA: New England Association for the Education of Young Children.

Gibran, Kahil. (1951). *The Prophet*. New York: Alfred A. Knopf, Publishers. Copyright renewed by Administrators C.T.A. of Kahil Gibran estate.

Heegaard, Marge. (1988). *When Someone Very Special Dies*. Minneapolis, MN: Woodland Press.

Heegaard, Marge. (1990). *When Mom and Dad Separate*. Minneapolis, MN: Woodland Press.

Heegaard, Marge. (1991). *When Someone Has a Very Serious Illness*. Minneapolis, MN: Woodland Press.

Hoban, Tana. (1971). *Look Again*. New York, NY: Macmillan Publishing Co.

Ives, Sally, David Fassler, & Michele Lash. (1985). *The Divorce Workbook: A Guide for Kids & Families*. Burlington, VT: Waterfront Books.

Jackson, Edgar. (1973). *Coping with the Crises in Your Life*. Northvale, NJ: Aronson, Jason Inc.

Kubler-Ross, Elizabeth (Ed.). (1975). *Death: The Final Stage of Growth*. Englewood Cliffs, NJ: Prentice-Hall, Inc.

Lombardo, Victor S. and Edith Lombardo. (1986). *Kids Grieve Too*. Springfield, IL: C. C. Thomas.

Mellonie, Bryan and Robert Ingpen. (1983). *Liftimes: The Beautiful Way to Explain Death to Children*. New York, NY: Bantam books.

Moser, Adolph. (1988). *Don't Pop Your Cork on Monday.* Kansas City, MO: Landmark Editions.

Nelson, Vacinda. (1988). *Always Grandma.* New York, NY: South China Printing Co.

Oaklander, Violet. (1969). *Windows to Our Children: Gestalt Therapy for Children.* New York, NY: Center for Gestalt Development.

O'Toole, Donna. (1989). *Growing through Grief: A K-12 Curriculum to HELP Young People through All Kinds of Loss.* Burnsville, NC: Mt. Rainbow Publications.

Quinlan, Patricia. (1987). *My Daddy Takes Care of Me.* Ontario, Canada: Annick Press.

Rogers, Fred. (1988). *When a Pet Dies.* New York: G. P. Putnam's Sons.

Rubenstein, Judith. (May 14, 1982). Preparing a Child for a Good-bye Visit to a Dying Loved One. *Journal of the American Medical Association* (JAMA), *247,* 2571–2572.

Sanford, Doris. (1985). *It Must Hurt a Lot.* Portland, OR: Multnomah Press.

Sanford, Doris. (1985). *Please Come Home.* Portland, OR: Multnomah Press.

Sanford, Doris. (1986). *I Can't Talk About It.* Portland, OR: Questar Publishers, Multnomah Press.

Silverstein, Shel. (1974). *Where the Sidewalk Ends.* New York, NY: HarperCollins Publishers.

Stein, Sarah. (1974). *About Dying.* New York, NY: Walker and Co.

Trout, Susan. (1990). *To See Differently.* Washington, DC: Three Roses Press.

Viorst, Judith. (1972). *Alexander and the Terrible Horrible No Good Very Bad Day.* New York: Aladdin Books.

Viorst, Judith. (1992). *The Good-Bye Book.* New York, NY: Aladdin Books.

Weiner, Lori. (September, 1991). Women and Human Immunodeficiency Virus: A historical and personal psychological perspective. *Social Work, 36* (5), 375–378.

White, E.B. (1952). *Charlotte's Web.* New York, NY: Harper Row.

Wolfelt, Alan. (1983). *Helping Children Cope with Grief.* Muncie, IN: Accelerated Development Inc.

Wolfelt, Alan. (Summer 1992). *Centerpiece* newsletter. Fort Collins, CO: The Center for Loss and Life Transition.

ABOUT THE AUTHOR

Linda Goldman is the author of *Breaking the Silence: A Guide To Help Children With Complicated Grief: Suicide, Homicide, AIDS, and Abuse* and *Bart Speaks Out On Suicide: Helping The Grieving Children in the School*. She has been an educator in the public school system as a teacher and counselor for almost 20 years.

Presently Linda is a certified grief therapist and certified grief educator practicing near Washington, DC. An innovative grief therapist, Linda began her private grief practice after the death of her stillborn daughter, Jennifer. Working with grieving children, teenagers, and adults, Linda finds gentle and creative ways to work through the sensitive feelings and thoughts associated with loss and grief issues. She was acknowledged by the Washington Magazine as one of the top therapists in the Washington, DC, Virginia, and Maryland area.

The success of her grief work has led her to educate other caring adults through training in school systems and universities, including Johns Hopkins Graduate School and University of Maryland School of Social Work/Advanced Certification Program for Children and Adolescents, sharing diverse ways of working with children and grief, and as acting a panelist for the National Teleconference "When A Parent Dies: Helping The Child." She also serves on the board of the American Death Education and Counseling Association (ADEC). Linda lives in Chevy Chase, MD, with her husband, Michael, and her son, Jonathan.

Index

Silverstein, Shel, 17
Spirituality, 27
Stillborn babies, 32
Story telling, 62, 73
Stranger anxiety or elective mutism, 182
Suicide
    books about, 184–185
    secrecy about, 77

T

Tape recorders, 94
Teachable moments
    elements of, 117–118
    techniques for, 119–122
Tears In Heaven, *98*
To See Differently (Trout), 32
Toddlers, 31. *See also* Children
Traditional rituals, 25
Trainings, 145–146
Trauma, 186
Trout, Susan, 32

U

"Uncle Bryan is a Flower Blooming" (Feikin), 45
Understanding
    blocked by common cliches, 40–41

developmental stages of childhood, 42–43
effected by magical thinking, 39
explanation of, 38

V

Video resources, 171
Violence
    books about, 185–186
    children's reaction to, 120–122
    exposure to, 3, 20
    help for children experiencing, 21
    prevalence of, 2

W

Websites, 172–173
Weight disorders, 182
Weiner, Lori, 62
When Dinosaurs Die (Brown), 119
Windows To Our Children (Oaklander), 56
Withdrawal, 59
Wolfelt, Alan, 24, 31
Working parents, 187
Worry boxes, 78
Writing, 44